Heaven Can't Wait

Heaven Can't Wait

◄§ SERMONS FOR THE YOUNG IN SPIRIT

by Peter Marshall

Edited and with Introductions by
Catherine Marshall

Preface by Peter J. Marshall

Published by
√chosen books
Lincoln, Virginia 22078
Distributed by Word Books • Waco, Texas 76703

HEAVEN CAN'T WAIT

Library of Congress Catalog Card Number: 63-20813

ISBN 0–912376–44–9

To the Risen Christ,
Peter Marshall's "Chief,"
the Living Inspiration
for these words

ACKNOWLEDGMENTS

It is never possible to complete a book manuscript without the encouragement, the advice, and the help of many people. I am grateful to Miss Patricia Harris, my secretary, who for many months went far beyond the call of duty in typing and retyping this manuscript; to my husband, Leonard Earl LeSourd, who first conceived the idea for this book, whose enthusiasm for Peter Marshall's material is unflagging, and whose editorial knowledge has been invaluable; to my son, Peter John Marshall, who has made many valuable suggestions; to friends who have been generous in permitting me to use some of their reminiscences of Dr. Marshall: Miss Jean Tucker, the Reverend Mr. J. David Simpson, Mr. David Kerr, Mr. Willard Daughtry, Marguerite Barze (Mrs. Roland Barze).

*

CONTENTS

PREFACE

It has been fourteen years since the death of my father, and now I am preparing at Princeton Seminary to go into the ministry. I am being guided to carry out Christ's ministry to men not so much to follow in my father's footsteps as to follow in the footsteps of the Lord he served.

Because one of my greatest hopes for this book is that the youth of America will read it, and because I am myself only recently out of my teen-age and college years, it is perhaps fitting that I briefly give you my perspective on these dozen sermons of my father.

I have always had difficulty separating what I remember about my father from what I have been told about him. Like most PKs (preachers' kids), I didn't see as much of my father as I would have desired. Since he died when I was only nine, my recollections of him are somewhat hazy. This meant that I didn't really begin to appreciate my father's ministry and his relationship with his "Chief" until I had embarked on my own relationship with this same Lord.

Young people in postwar America have grown up in the disillusioning knowledge that the world is no longer "safe for democracy," or for that matter safe for much of anything. It is not hard to see the reason for this when we are being honest with ourselves—man has never, cannot now, and will not be able in the future to control completely his own destiny. This knowledge tends these days to make young people cynical. Why? Because all children grow up with their hearts full of ideals, but the youth of postwar America have also grown up with their eyes full of the chaos of the society that adults are handing on to them to manage. This combination has produced cynicism in young people, for cynics are really those who have become disillusioned by the seeming impossibility of their idealism.

America has become fascinated lately with an introspective psychoanalysis of the problems of youth in our society. Americans have decided that today's teen-ager is really the victim of the anxieties of the Bomb and the Cold War, not unlike his parents. It is true that the mores of today's teen-ager are in reality only an emulation of those of his parents expressed in a slightly more exuberant manner. However, to decide that the problems of today's youth are also the problems of the world in which we live is to solve nothing. This merely dissipates the guilt by making it collective. The fact of the matter is that every person, whether youngster or parent, you or I, is responsible before God for his own conduct.

I suppose I rebelled against the Christian faith of my parents more than most children raised in a Christian home, probably because as Peter Marshall's son I was somewhat in the spotlight. However, when I had finished college and rebellion had soured, I found that I could see no purpose or direction for my life. It was at this time that I realized my youthful cynicism was not the fault of my parents, or the society of which I was a part, but solely a result of my refusal to accept the love of Christ and God's plan for my life. The seeds planted in me by my parents' faith had begun to sprout.

At this same time I saw what father was trying to say to all of us, or—perhaps better—what Christ was trying to say to all of us through father. One aspect of his sermons has always stood out in my mind, and I think it applies emphatically to the sermons in this book. His sermons are timeless. They have an eternal significance that not only strides back over the blow-

ing sands of man's past, but also rockets forward into the star-
lit void of man's future. Why? Why does the work of Peter
Marshall continue to stir the soul of man?

There are two answers, I think. First, because the questions
he asks here out of his concern for youth are the perpetual ones
of human existence—love and marriage, freedom and responsibility, honesty and deception, faith and hope, adventure and
destiny—in short, the meaning of life and death. Second, because he answered these eternal questions with the only eternal
response—God's abiding Word to man, the burning light that
Christ's love for man sheds into a world of darkness.

Only Christ's love can free us from the necessity of clutching
at material possessions. A marriage, a beautiful home, a good
job, and two cars in the garage do not make happiness! But
God's love can convert the disillusioned into disciples of the
Idealist whose ideals come true in the lives of men. This is the
message of these sermons to all men, especially to youth.

My father had a great love for this country, which I share.
Now it seems as though America has sold its ancient Puritan
birthright—the possibility of a nation that is great because of
its relationship to its Lord—for cocktail parties and expense-
account lunches. How long are we going to watch ourselves
become, in T. S. Eliot's words,

... the hollow men
... the stuffed men
Leaning together
Headpiece filled with straw. Alas!

Our problem is not really communism, nor is it bigness in
government, nor any of the other issues that fill the headlines.
It is ourselves and our love of self. There is only one answer for
us, and it is an answer for each individual heart. Only when
we accept Christ's love for us, and enter into a daily relation-

ship with Him, can we be freed from the chains of selfishness that bind us.

I hope that you will find, as I have, that the only Reality in life starts with the Reality that is Jesus Christ. This is the good news Peter Marshall proclaimed in every sermon—the Risen Christ.

Peter J. Marshall

Princeton, N.J.
June 1963

INTRODUCTION

≈§ Why should there be another book of Peter Marshall's sermons?

Mr. Jones, Meet the Master, which came out in the autumn of 1949, nine months after Peter's death, used only twelve sermons out of six hundred complete manuscripts. In *A Man Called Peter* other sermons were referred to, with brief excerpts from fourteen quoted. And in *The First Easter*, Peter's Easter material was collected and edited into a sermon-narrative of the last days of Christ on this earth. Apparently these books only served to arouse greater and greater interest in Dr. Marshall's ministry, for, through the years, there has been a never-ceasing stream of requests for more. Many of these requests have come from teen-agers:

> *I am wondering if I could have copies of the four sermons listed below? I ask you this because I have read small passages from them, and I long to see the rest.*
> *I know this is an awful lot to ask . . . I am a freshman in college. . . . I was so far away from God, but because of what Peter Marshall has taught me about the joy of the Christian life, I am happy to tell you that this is no longer the case. . . .*

While the sermons in this book should be of special interest to the young, the book is not directed exclusively to them. It could not be—because Peter Marshall never segregated young people, never talked down to them or patronized them. He expected the most of the younger members of his congregations and he got it—by paying them the compliment of treating them as adults. Conversely, he made the old people in his congregations feel young in spirit, and they loved him for it.

The hunger in young people today for answers (implicit in letters like the one above) is something to remember as we read our newspapers and periodicals so full of the "teen-age problem." That there is a problem, a deep and serious one, few thoughtful persons would question. Yet my experience has been that many of these young people are seriously seeking resolutions to the puzzles in their lives and are scorning saccharine or superficial answers. Something about the temper of our time has given them an eleventh-hour consciousness. They want the truth—even when it hurts.

The truth was what Peter Marshall always gave them. Perhaps that is one reason why during his lifetime and afterward when his sermons and prayers were published, the young in heart have clamored for more of the man, his ideas, his wisdom. This book's former title, *John Doe, Disciple*, is taken from one of his sermons. It is meant to challenge: would you, John Doe, be a disciple today were Christ to reappear? Would you have the courage? Would you make the sacrifices?

My initial impressions of Peter Marshall come from my own teen-age years. It was during the autumn of my sophomore year at Agnes Scott in Decatur, Georgia, that the name Peter Marshall kept cropping up in dormitory talkfests. It was obvious that the young bachelor Scotsman had captured the imagination of the college girls.

Finally, my curiosity aroused, I went with a group of them to the Westminster Presbyterian Church in Atlanta to hear him. I still remember what a production it was to get there— a minimum of forty-five minutes each way by slow streetcar.

But it was worth the effort. My friends had not exaggerated. He was young, with unruly curly hair, the build of a football player under his Geneva gown, and a strong Scots burr. More important, Peter Marshall preached to us of a red-blooded living Lord. I had never heard preaching quite like that, and I—along with hundreds of other young people from Atlanta's five major colleges and universities—was drawn back again and again.

I was aware of intriguing contrasts in this young minister: intense earnestness, and an irrepressible sense of humor; rugged manliness alongside a poetic sensitivity; idealism with touches of earthiness. We college students felt that he spoke our language. Yet he could also lift the King's English to a dignity and beauty at times lyrical, sometimes Shakesperian . . . at moments (for me, anyway) Churchillian. Outside the church he could exhibit exuberant playfulness, but in the pulpit a mantle of power and dignity fell upon him.

After Peter and I were married, I soon found that there was a sense in which he was younger than I, though chronologically he was twelve years older. Peter would still be fresh at 1 or 2 A.M., long after I had wilted. He could outdance me, outplay me, exhibit a bounding physical vitality I never had. Nor did this change through the years. He was bowling on the night before his first heart attack. He was out for an evening of recreation with three men friends on the night before he died.

In Washington during the second world war, some of the old-timers at the New York Avenue Presbyterian Church were afraid that the staid and historic church with its dignified pulpit was turning into a youth center. Girls had poured into the nation's capital from every section of the country for government jobs. There were always servicemen, WAVES, and WACS in the city on leave. A steady procession of all these young people came through the church. There were 125 young voices in Charlie Beaschler's chorus-choir. There was a canteen. There was a Sunday-school class which Peter Marshall taught for many years. There was a Sunday-evening youth service. Busloads of girls from private schools came to the regular Sunday-morning service. It must have seemed to the old-timers that the foyers, the Lecture Room, the Lincoln Room were overrun with noisy youngsters.

Peter gloried in this. He felt that he knew how mothers and fathers in little towns in Ohio, Iowa, or Kansas would feel about their sons and daughters having found a home away from home centered in the encircling arms of the church.

His hold on these young people was not just that of a speaker to whom they enjoyed listening. He bowled with them on one of the church's four teams in a city-wide league. A group usually went with him to a small newsreel theater near the church after the informal midweek service. Of a Sunday evening—after a day of speaking three times, sometimes four —he always felt the need to unwind. Usually at the close of the service, a group would be patiently waiting to help him relax. He kept a supply of games—Parchesi, Rook, Chess, Sorry, Yacht—in his church office. Even after such a grueling day, he could outlast any of his youthful opponents.

His relationship with young people was characterized by familiarity, but never disrespect. They could call their minister "Peter" if they wanted to, but never "Doc" or "Pete"—both of which he disliked. There were no off-color jokes told in his presence. He held them to their highest and they loved him for it.

After his death, one young man wrote me, "I used to look forward to our Sunday evenings last year. I enjoyed the chess games, but I especially prized the chance for informal conversations and sociability with Peter."

Another reminisced, "He lived what he believed, but never with long-faced piety. He did everything from fishing or going to baseball games to preaching with such delight and devotion that he made it seem a high adventure. You enjoyed things with Peter by proxy. . . . I received Peter's preaching with all the eagerness of a hungry man for a square meal. His powerful messages burned deep into my soul and became the very foundation for what I believe today.

"Yet my friendship with him had another, equally wonderful side: Helping him to do the wiring and the layout for an elaborate electric train. . . . Sharing with him the making of an amateur movie travelogue of Washington. . . . A trip with him and two other men to New York where we had a dizzy round of radio shows, musical comedies, the opera, and numerous restaurants. Perhaps it was because he took Christ into his recreation that it was such fun to be with him."

A reporter who came to the New York Avenue Church for an interview-story one day, pointing out the roomful of young people in the downstairs church office, said to Peter Marshall, "We are hearing a lot about the godlessness of modern youth. Do you think these kids will get into heaven?"

Peter's answer was decisive. "All I know is—if they *don't* get to heaven, then I want to be where they go."

Catherine Marshall

Chappaqua, N.Y.
June 1, 1963

·I·

≈§ *If ever a man felt himself guided by direct communication with his Lord, that man was Peter Marshall. To me he seemed Exhibit A of God's ability to guide His children in our day quite as well as He did in centuries long gone.*

"Look at me," Peter's presence in the pulpit said; "if God had not led me, I might still be an engineer in Stewart and Lloyds Imperial Tube Works in Scotland."

It was a long way that God led him, with His hand apparent time after time. At twenty-one, Peter had volunteered to the London Missionary Society for service in China. That door was shut firmly. The way led not to the Orient but to the United States.

New Jersey—was that the place? Peter was miserable there. Within four months he knew that the next sealed order read Birmingham, Alabama.

Two months after Peter's arrival in the Southern city he was writing to a relative:

> I have found happiness at last. It is not a happiness of my job in the Circulation Department of the *Birmingham News*, though I like that very well. It is a deeper joy that has to be with numerous opportunities for service for the Lord. . . .
>
> It is romantic how things are happening. Dr. Mordecai, the minister of the church I have joined, says that he will do all in his power to put me into a theological

seminary next fall. He recognizes, as I do, that my voca-
tion in life is clearly the ministry. . . .

Indeed I was sent to Birmingham. Everything is
great! I am blessed beyond words. All the unhappiness I
had in New Jersey has only served to make me appreciate
this all the more. . . .

*Dr. Mordecai kept his pledge and Peter entered seminary
the following September. Still there was that continuing sense
of God's hand on his shoulder. After graduation, the little mill
town of Covington, Georgia, was his first pastorate, then
Atlanta. There his happiness and delight in his ministry could
scarcely have been greater.*

*Then in 1936 came the call to Washington, D.C. Peter
could not bear the thought of leaving Atlanta. Surely the time
was not yet, there was still so much to be done. So, flattering
though the offer was, he refused it. Eight months later the call
came again. This time there was no mistaking the by-now
familiar tap on the shoulder: his marching orders from his
Chief said Washington.*

*Through subsequent years there were tempting offers from
important churches in other cities—Baltimore, Pittsburgh, Dal-
las, Philadelphia, Tulsa, New York. On occasions the guidance
was not easy to get; there were times when he struggled and
strained to hear God's voice. But looking back now, I know
that he was guided aright. When a man intensely desires to
obey God's directions, somehow God manages to get through
to that man.*

*Peter received propositions of other types that tested this
matter of God's guidance. A famous New Orleans attorney,
while a naval commander during the second world war, began
coming to hear Peter Marshall preach. Eventually he made
Peter an astonishing offer: "If you will leave the ministry to*

become a criminal lawyer, my firm will pick up all the tabs on your legal education, provide abundantly for your family, take you into our firm to plead all important cases, guarantee you a beginning minimum salary of X dollars." Compared to the salary of any minister, it was a magnificent amount.

Peter was as flattered by this as anyone would have been. For a few days he flirted with the idea. But in this case, the answer was not difficult to hear. It was a clear, resounding "No, you know perfectly well that I called you to preach. You would never for one moment be really happy doing anything else."

The years sped by. On the morning of March 30, 1946, Peter suffered an unexpected and devastating heart attack. It looked as if it might well be the end of the road for him. But that was not God's plan. "I have a surprise for you," the message seemed to be. "Some of your most important work is still ahead." When on January 5, 1947, Peter was made chaplain of the United States Senate, it could scarcely have been more of a surprise. Eleven days later he wrote to a dear friend in typical Peter Marshall style:

> The whole thing came out of the blue. I agreed to accept it, if it came to me as a call from the Chief. So it did—and I could do no other than to accept it. . . .

The Senate Chaplaincy made the nation as a whole aware of Peter Marshall. This was important only in that it provided him with an ever-widening area of service for his Lord.

How wide that ministry would eventually be, Peter himself could never have guessed. For even as he was Exhibit A for the reality of God's guidance during his lifetime, so he would also be a prime example of the glory that can attend our transition into the next life and proof of how there can be no "losses" in God's planning.

I like to think that the next portion of the "sealed orders"

came to me. The gist of those orders was: "Peter's ministry is
not cut off by his death at all. You will see——"

I saw. I have had proof—glorious corroboration. In the
decade after his death millions of people who had never seen
Peter Marshall or heard him preach read his sermons and prayers as well as the story of his life.

Of course, God can guide your life and mine. And once
you have experienced this direct communication, you will not
want to live by any other Guide.

UNDER SEALED ORDERS

I do not know what picture the phrase under sealed orders
suggests to you.
To me it recalls very vividly a scene from the first world war,
when I was a little boy spending vacations at a Scottish seaport.

I saw a gray destroyer slipping hurriedly from port in response
to some urgent commands . . .
I watched the crew hurry their preparations for sailing,
        watched them cast off the mooring hawsers . . .
saw the sleek ship get under way, as she rose to meet the lazy
ground swell of a summer evening . . .
Her Morse lamp was winking on the control bridge aft, and I
watched her until she was lost in the mists of the North Sea.

She was a mystery vessel.
She had sailed under sealed orders.
Not even her officers knew her destination or the point of
rendezvous.

We all start out in life, going—we know not where.
It will be revealed later.
But meanwhile we must go out in faith—
                        under sealed orders.

So, in like manner, all the pioneers of faith have gone out—
and all the explorers—
        Abraham of old
            Columbus
                Magellan
                    John Smith
                        Peary
                            Lindbergh
                                Byrd.

Abraham stands out among the Old Testament heroes as the
leading example of this kind of faith.
In the Epistle to the Hebrews we are told:
        "By faith Abraham . . . went out, not knowing whither
        he went."   *Hebrews* 11:8

Here was Abraham, a mature and successful man, having
established himself in Ur of the Chaldees.
Then God spoke to him:
        "Get thee out of thy country, and from thy kindred, and
        from thy father's house, unto a land that I will shew
        thee: And I will make of thee a great nation, and I will
        bless thee, and make thy name great . . . and in thee shall
        all families of the earth be blessed."   *Genesis* 12:1–3

Try to imagine what was involved in obeying this guidance.
Abraham had to sever all his business connections,
                        uproot himself,
procure supplies for a new and strange way of life.
He was giving up the comforts and conveniences of a world
he knew to live as a nomad under canvas with no settled abode.

From a commonsense point of view, it was crazy.
Doubtless Abraham had many friends who told him just that.
Where was he going?
Well, he did not know exactly.
What was he going to do?
He was going to found a new nation somewhere else.
Found a new nation?
What was he talking about?

He and his wife did not even have any children, and they were getting on in years.
Abraham himself was seventy-five!
What kind of crazy talk was that?

Nevertheless Abraham carried out his decision.
He left Ur of the Chaldees.
He did it because of a spiritual insight—an insight which for him had the authority of a direct command from God.

And God kept His part of the bargain.
Abraham was led to Canaan.
In their old age, he and his wife Sarah had a son—Isaac.
"I will multiply thy seed as the stars of the heaven . . . and in thy seed shall all the nations of the earth be blessed," God had promised.

And it came to pass.
For this pioneer of faith became the father of the Hebrew nation.
And through him, all men everywhere have been blessed—for Jesus Christ Himself was to be one of Abraham's descendants.

Some people find it difficult to believe that human beings like us, like Abraham, can get direct guidance from God,
can have their lives ordered by Him.

They ask, "But surely you don't believe that
God speaks directly
    specifically
as I am speaking to you now?
You don't mean that God sends telegrams?

Now the Bible always speaks of God saying to His children this
and that . . . "And God said unto Abraham . . ."
            "God said unto Moses. . . ."
Was that just for Bible times?

If you have never had an experience of God's guidance in your
life, you may question how it comes.
No doubt it comes in various ways to different people.
I cannot fully explain it, but I have to believe it, because I have
had many experiences of God's guidance which were for me
just as dramatic and critical as the guidance that came to
Abraham.

I was given an opportunity to leave Scotland and come to this
country, and I asked God what I should do about it.
I asked God in the only way we have to ask Him—through
prayer.
I prayed and waited for the answer.

I believed that the answer would come; I did not know when
or how.
For three weeks I waited with some impatience, I must con-
fess, and at the end of that time, the answer came, and God
told me to go.

I could not accurately describe what was a subjective experience.
I did not see the answer written in the sky, nor yet upon the
wall of my room.

But I knew—positively, definitely, that God had said, "Yes, go."

I remember well the spot where the answer came.

It was on a beautiful Sunday afternoon outside Glasgow.

I was walking down a path lined with rhododendron on the Sholto-Douglas estate when I heard the voice.

Now, whether it sounded like a voice outside of me or inside of me, I cannot tell.

But I knew it was the voice of God.

I was positive that the answer for which I had prayed had come, and I acted upon it immediately by making application for a visa to enter the United States as a quota immigrant.

Well do I remember on the nineteenth of March, 1927, standing on the afterdeck of the *Cameronia*, watching with moist eyes the purple hills of Mull of Kintyre sinking beneath the screw-threshed waters of the Atlantic, when every turn of the propeller was driving me farther from the land of my birth—from all I knew and loved.

And then—I walked slowly and wonderingly for'ard until I was leaning over the prow.

I stood looking into the west,

wondering what lay beyond that tumbling horizon—

wondering what the unknown tomorrow held for me.

I, too, was going out in faith, not knowing whither I went.

I was leaving the tube mill, where I had been working in the machine shop.

I was coming to the United States to enter the ministry, because I believed with all my heart that those were my orders from my Chief.

But I did not know how,

or when

or where.

I could not foresee the wonderful way in which God would open doors of opportunity.

I could never have imagined the thrilling way in which God was to arrange my life . . .

order my ways

guide my steps

provide for all my needs

give me wonderful friends, generous helpers

until, at last, I would achieve His plan for me, and be ordained a minister of the Gospel.

It is an amazing adventure simply to be born upon this wandering island in the sky, to make a temporary home on this rolling ball of matter . . .

To go to school

    to make friends

      to marry

        to choose a career and to develop it,

to rear children and assume life's responsibilities;

to face life with its swift changes of circumstances that no man can certainly predict an hour ahead—

    These are all adventures.

And it is an adventure to leave it when death calls and "Taps" sounds for you at the close of life's day.

Each new day is like an hitherto unvisited country which we enter—like Abraham leaving Ur for a strange land—

    "not knowing whither he went."

And every new year we begin a tour of exploration into twelve months where no man's foot has ever walked before.

If we all love tales of pioneers, it is because from the time we are weaned until the time we die—life is pioneering.

With all his science, with all his new insights and tools for conquering the unknown, man must face each day as Paul faced

his journey to Rome—"not knowing the things that shall be-
fall him there."

As you stand peering into the future—you cannot see what
tomorrow will bring.
You cannot even tell as you look upon Grandfather Time
whether his indistinct features are smiling or frowning . . .
And his hand behind his back—does it hold a bouquet
                                              or a brickbat?

Is there no way, then, that we can know the future?
Shall we go—you and I—to some wizened old hag, cross her
palm with silver, and permit her to spread fanlike before us a
deck of cards so that she may tell us what the future holds?
Shall we listen to her as she interprets a fair lady or a dark
knave as the message of a deuce or a trey?

Can it be that the drawing of a card will signify
the career we shall follow,
        or the girl we shall marry,
            or the family we shall have?
Nonsense!
There are so many things that even the most educated among
us do not know!
Things that no faculty can teach us . . .
        that no textbooks can contain . . .
            that no man can foresee or prophesy.

I urge you then simply to go out in faith—even as Abraham
                                Columbus
                    or the Pilgrim Fathers
and all the host of pioneers of the centuries.

Yet this is not easy.
Today we must send young people into a changing world

where old concepts are being discarded,
   old theories exploded,
      where standards are constantly changing—
into this unknown they must go, whether they like it or not.

But then is everything so uncertain, you ask?
Is there nothing on which I can rely?

Yes, there is an assurance that can help you to confidently and
successfully face the unknown vistas of all the tomorrows.
It is an assurance given to us in the old Book:

"But I trusted in Thee, O Lord:
I said, Thou art my God.
My times are in Thy hand."   *Psalm* 31:14–15

If you trust in God, if you are willing to give your life to Him,
then, and only then, will you have no fear.
For no matter where you go, He will be with you.
You can never wander from the pathway, for He will lead you.

Some people speak of *luck* and accord it a great and determin-
ing place in their lives.
                  They trust to luck,
                     they count on it, live by it.
                  They cross their fingers, knock on wood,
                     look for four-leaf clovers and carry rabbits' feet.
But I would not dare wish you or anyone else "Luck"
because there is no such thing as luck!
Others speak of "accidents"—and make allowance for the happening of accidents—regard certain events as purely accidental.
Yet are there really such things as accidents?

Was the creation of the world an accident?
Are the laws that maintain the universe accidental?
Ask Eddington

or Jeans
  or Milliken
    or Einstein.

Were the prophecies of the Old Testament accidental?
Was the birth of Jesus Christ an accident?
It was no accident that Judas printed the kiss of betrayal on the
fair cheek of Jesus!
The old Rugged Cross was no accident!
Paul's conversion was not an accident!
The work of Martin Luther was no accident!

Was it an accident that John and Charles Wesley were rescued
from a burning house, as they themselves described it, "like
brands from the burning"?

Is this nation of ours an accident?
Were George Washington and the Declaration of Independence,
  Abraham Lincoln and the Emancipation Proclamation
purely accidental?
Is a rose an accident—merely the coming together of capricious
factors in nature?

I shall not soon forget the words of Dr. W. R. Whitney, a past
President of the American Chemical Society,
  Fellow of the American Academy of Arts and Sciences,
    director of many vast electrical researches, as he made
    the simplest of all experiments.

Dr. Whitney picked up from his desk a small bar magnet.
He brought this near a steel needle, and the needle leaped to
the magnet.
Why?
Dr. Whitney said:

"We have worked out elaborate explanations.
We speak learnedly of lines of force.
We draw a diagram of the magnetic field.

"Yet we know that there are no lines there and the *field* is just a word to cover our ignorance.
Our explanations are only educated guesses.

"Or consider," Dr. Whitney continued, "the beam of light that comes speeding from a star, traveling hundreds of years. Finally it reaches your optic nerve, and you *see* the star.

"How does that happen?
We have our corpuscular theory of light,
      our wave theory,
          our quantum theory.
But they are all just educated guesses.

"So," explained Dr. Whitney, "after we are all finished with our theories and our guesses, we are still backed up against the fact of God—the will of God at work in what we call 'science.'"

Thus an eminent scientist looks beyond science (that some still think infallible and the source of all answers) for guidance.

Many of our scientific theories and explanations are only educated guesses.
The day before yesterday, the atom was thought of as whirling particles but that is outmoded now.
Yesterday the atom was described as a wave in space, according to Schrödinger's theory; that too is outmoded.

Today the atom has been split and developed into the greatest explosive force in the history of mankind.
No, the theory of relativity is not final.
No scientific concept stands still.

All is in motion, because we are forever in the process of discovering more of what God has placed in this world.

But the will of God, the laws we discover
                 but cannot always understand
                 or explain,
the will of God alone is final.

No there are no accidents.
God is still the ruler of His universe and of our lives,
                                 yours and mine.

So, even though you go out, not knowing whither you go,
                 you can go confidently, like Abraham,
provided you can say with the Psalmist:
     "My times are in Thy hand."

God knows each one of you, and He has a plan for *you*.
God made one you—and only one.
Nobody who ever lived was quite as you are now.
God gave you life for a purpose, and if you fail to fulfill it, that purpose will never be realized.

I long for all you young people to know the full fellowship of the Christian life . . .
     what it is to be guided by the Lord into the very place
     where He wants you to be . . .
          to know when you make decisions that you are doing
          what He wants you to do.

Not only ministers can find God's will; so too can clerks
                                 and secretaries
                              and engineers
                              and waitresses
                              and salesmen
                           and bus drivers.

If you only knew the peace that comes with the conviction that you are in the place where God wants you to be ... and that you are doing the thing for which He created you.
What a difference it makes!

To Abraham, God spoke directly and specifically.
Nowadays, since the advent of Jesus Christ, I believe that God speaks to you and me through the Holy Spirit.
Indeed, we are told in the Scriptures that it is the function of the Holy Spirit to guide us,
    to lead us into all truth.

So the Holy Spirit is available to guide us in everything:
    A young man into his life work,
        A young woman into the friendship out of which will grow love and marriage to the man of God's choice for her.
            A family can be led to the city where God wants them to live ...
                A businessman can be guided to make the right decisions.

No, that is not silly, it is not fanaticism.
Nor does it do violence to human responsibility.
As soon as you try living this way, you will find that God's purpose for your life is maximum creativity, achievement, and responsibility—not less.

Others object to the idea that the Lord of the universe could possibly be concerned about the details of millions of lives.
Yet this glorious truth could never have been imagined.
Jesus said it was so, and He would never raise false hopes in a human heart.

Jesus' emphasis was always upon the one—the single soul.
Consider His parables—the story of the lost coin,

of the one lost sheep,
and of the lone lost boy.

"... the very hairs of your head are all numbered," He
said.   *Matthew* 10:30
"... your Heavenly Father knoweth that ye have need of
all these *things*."   *Matthew* 6:32

In this viewpoint, Jesus was being realistic about human life.
The truth is that our lives are made up of the sum of
the small decisions
the little turnings
the minute choices.
If we do not let God into these everyday details, practically
speaking we are not letting Him in at all.

Would you like to have God's guidance for your life?
If you would, first you have to believe that He can guide you.

But faith is not belief.
Faith is belief plus what you do with that belief.

I might have believed intellectually that God could guide me,
indeed, that I had heard His voice that afternoon in the park.
But that would have counted for nothing, had I not gone on
to act on that belief by applying for my number as a quota
immigrant.
Belief becomes faith only at the point of action.

First of all, if you want to hear God, you will have to face up
squarely to the question,
"Am I willing to follow His plan wherever it may lead?"
"Am I willing to do whatever He tells me to do?"

This is a decision that must be resolved before you can receive
any guidance from God,
before your Christian adventure can begin.

How hard it is for our proud wills to bow the neck and call
Him "Master and Lord"!
Yet bow we must, if we are to understand what life is all about,
if we are to take even the first step toward maturity,

                         or fulfillment,
                         or greatness.

Understand that this is no craven slavery Christ asks of us:
    "Henceforth I call you not servants; for the servant
    knoweth not what his lord doeth; but I have called you
    friends . . ."   *John 15:15*

A friend of Jesus!
No knight of old ever had a greater privilege.
He who bows before This One—joyously to hand over his life
and his future—
    finds himself raised to knighthood,
      received into the inner circle,
        immediately heir to all the rights and privileges of
        the King.

But the move is ours . . .
Are you willing to tell God now that you will follow His plan
wherever it may lead?

This is important because God has given us free will, and this
He will never violate.
He holds in a more profound respect than any of us could the
sanctity of every human personality.
Therefore He requires the consent of our wills before He will
enter our hearts and lives.

And it is just at this point that many of us are in the grip of a
terrible conflict:
We want to hear God speaking to us . . .
    but we are afraid of what we might hear.

We want to be made clean . . .
    but there is still a hunger for the husks the swine eat.
We would follow Christ . . .
    but we don't want our friends to think us queer.
We want God's way . . .
    but we also want our own way.

There is an answer to our dilemma . . .
Tell Christ honestly about our divided will . . .
            our divided self.
Ask Him to take that over and make it whole.
And He will!

It may be that His plan for you will not be revealed for some time.
You will have to keep close to Him, keep listening for His signals.
His plan for you may be a gradual development.

There are a thousand ways in which He may use you.
You may have to make some changes in your life,
        break with some of your present companions,
       change some of your habits . . .
I cannot tell you that—but He can.

He will send His power surging into you,
       to give you power to defeat temptations,
     to chase away your fears,
    to give you a quiet heart,
   to make you joyous and free.

We are living in a hazardous epoch of history.
The wind . . . the earthquake . . . and the fire of old are here, in fact the threat of more terrible fire than man ever thought possible.

It would be tragedy indeed if the still, small voice of God's wisdom and direction is not heard at such a time.

You are leaving port under sealed orders and in a troubled period.

You cannot know whither you are going or what you are to do.

But why not take a Pilot on board who knows the nature of your sealed orders from the outset,

and who will shape your entire voyage accordingly?

He knows the shoals and the sandbanks,

the rocks and the reefs.

He will steer you safely into that celestial habor where your anchor will be cast for eternity.

Let His mighty nail-pierced hands hold the wheel, and you will be safe.

Now is a splendid time to entrust your life to Him, *now, as you begin.*

Give Him your life.

He will treasure it, even as you.

Then, though you may not know what will be your harbor, you will know your Pilot . . .

And all will be well.

·II·

◄§ *The letter from the young girl read in part:*

I smoke, I drink, I have sex with boys. My family does not seem to know – or at least don't appear to know – that I do all these things.

But are parents deaf and dumb? You may as well know why I can't take part in church affairs anymore. Maybe I'm a good girl, but I feel bad. I can't pray.

Sometimes after an exceedingly wild party I drop on my knees and say, "Oh God, forgive us all." You understand my crowd is not tough—just the boys and girls of the best families I was brought up with.

What puzzles me is the older people all saying that they have faith in us. . . . You preachers standing around telling us how fine and good we are. Sometime I'd like to kidnap you and take you on one of our parties. I guess your next sermon after that would be about sin. And that's what we need to hear.

Here are some of my questions:

Did my mother do the things I'm doing? Did my older sisters? Am I wrong in thinking that I am a bad girl? Is that the way of the world? Shall we go to heaven or to hell following such acts? Does God care? Do you preachers know that we young people do these things?

Please write something to quiet my mind, or I shall go mad.

It was to answer this letter that Peter Marshall preached "Heaven Can't Wait."

HEAVEN CAN'T WAIT

EACH one of you has a philosophy of life.
You may not realize it . . .
You may not even know it, but you have one nevertheless.

It may be sound—or it may be false.
It may be positive—or it may be negative.
It may be Christian—or it may be pagan.
Perhaps you could not expound it in so many words,
    but you have one just the same.

It lies back of every decision you make . . .
    It colors every opinion you hold . . .
It suggests every action you take . . .
            and it shows itself in a hundred different ways:
                The type of amusements you seek . . .
                The kind of pictures you prefer . . .
                The magazines and newspapers you read . . .
                The television programs you watch . . .
                The slang you use . . .
                Your favorite songs . . .

All these things are indicative of the tenor of your thinking and are clues to your philosophy of life.

Such a clue, I believe, is the title of a song of some years ago,
"Heaven Can Wait."
It is indicative of a prevailing idea to which a great many of
us subscribe . . .
"This is paradise enough" is a philosophy which says,
"We're only young once, let us have our fun while we can.
There's plenty of time for responsibility and serious
thoughts.
We're not ready to settle down yet . . .
We're out for a good time, so don't be a wet blanket by asking
us to be serious.
This is the time to be gay—so come along, let's dance.
Have another drink . . . you're only young once."

This idea is not new, nor is it modern.
You and your parents and your grandparents have been saying
it down through the ages.
Always there have been young people who have fallen victims
to this pagan philosophy and have expressed it in many different ways.

It was this idea that Robert Herrick expressed in the seven-
teenth century when he said:

> "Gather ye rosebuds while ye may,
>   Old Time is still a-flying:
> And this same flower that smiles to-day,
>   To-morrow will be dying."

You see, there is nothing new about the idea of sloughing off
of responsibilities or duties
    or thoughts of a future life.
There is nothing new here—but there is also nothing good
about it.

I wonder why it is that so many young people are afraid of
that which is high—afraid of high ideals
of high thoughts
of high morality.

Is it because so many grew up in homes saturated with cynicism
and helplessness
and defeatism
now that we have a bomb of such awesome destructiveness?

Some of you grew up in an age when not only big sisters and
brothers—but fathers and mothers took to drinking and stay-
ing out nights . . .
When young girls were trained to serve liquor in barrooms no
better than the old saloon . . .
When American women were persuaded by brilliant advertis-
ing that it was fashionable to drink . . .
When Hollywood and Freudian psychology were making us
sex-conscious as never before.

It is not surprising, therefore, that so many of you young people
have lost your moorings . . .
are confused and bewildered . . .
And have the feeling that no one—not even God—
cares about you.

Yet behind the "so what" indifference—the cynicism, the
boredom, all of you want challenges and jobs.
All of you want to make your own way in life . . .
unless you have been softened and spoiled by parental indulgence.

Most of you want to get married—and deeply and sincerely
desire your marriage to be a success . . .

You want to have a home and a family
  and you want to see some light ahead for your children.

You would like to give yourself to something worthwhile,
  perhaps a hospital project ...
    work with children ...
      the church.
Inside are stirrings and longings and a hunger for the real
meaning of life.
You are in search of happiness but don't know where to find
it, or even how to look.

So meanwhile you say, "Let's not worry or think about it.
Turn on the record player, and fill the room with jazz.
Live for today, do what comes naturally ...
This doesn't take thought,
    or hard work,
      or being different.
      "Heaven can wait."
But will young people, by postponing serious thoughts and re-
fusing to think of spiritual things, eventually stumble upon
some satisfying beliefs?
Will you one day—without thinking about it—find a satisfy-
ing experience of God?

Will you manage to find the happiness you seek by drifting
along, day by day, "gathering rosebuds while you may"?
Is it true that "Heaven can wait"?
    Does Heaven wait?
  Will Heaven wait?

Youth is the period of the most important decisions of life for
which the Lord's guidance is particularly needed.
It is in youth that we form our basic ideals and philosophies ...

It is in youth that we come to crossroads where decisions are
made between right and wrong:
>To do homework—or to sneak out the sexy magazine . . .
>To take a low grade—or cheat . . .
>And when caught doing something wrong to tell the truth
>fearlessly—or lie cravenly—
perhaps even shifting the blame to someone else.

These are the crossroads . . .
Here is where greatness begins its journey
>or weakness and evil take over.

Habits are begun in youth that solidify like concrete:
>Putting off assignments until it is too late . . .
>Telling litttle lies that grow into bigger lies
>>>that trap
>>>enmesh
>>>entwine
>>>imprison . . .
Giving away a priceless treasure a little at a time until it is all
gone, and you are soiled, distraught, bitter,
>and desperately disillusioned that love can turn so dirty . . .
Choosing friends that help lift your thinking,
>or lower it by feeding your ego, tempting you to do the
>things that deep inside you know are wrong.

It is in youth that we decide upon a life work.
Either we just drift into something as the only thing we could
get, or we carefully prepare at home and in school for that
niche in life which we feel is specifically ours.
But whether we drift or whether we steer a direct course, we
achieve that place we choose in youth.

It is usually in youth that we select a life partner.
And in this, the most important decision of our whole life,
we need the help and guidance of a Wisdom greater than our
own.

The prophet promised that it was the young who would see
visions . . .
    the old who would dream their dreams.

Joan of Arc was only seventeen when she was riding at the
head of the army that liberated France from the English.

John Calvin was twenty-six when he published his *Institutes*.
John Keats died at twenty-six . . .
Shelley was thirty when he was drowned, leaving English
literature his undying *Odes* . . .

Sir Isaac Newton had largely discovered the workings of the
law of gravitation when he was twenty-three . . .
Henry Clay was sent to the United States Senate at twenty-
nine, and was Speaker of the House of Representatives at
thirty-four . . .

Raphael painted his most important pictures between twenty-
five and thirty—he died at thirty-seven.
Van Dyck had done his best work before he was thirty.

Jesus Christ was not quite thirty-three when He died.
For the most part, His followers were young men.

Those who gathered at Pentecost were young people . . .
The movement that started when the winds of the Holy Spirit
blew through the streets of old Jerusalem was essentially a
youth movement.
It is for all these reasons, you see, that Heaven can't wait.
The visions that are to be granted are given to youth.

But voices that are unheeded have a way of being heard no more.
And visions that shine through the fogs and above the mists have a way of fading and disappearing as time goes oozing out.

"Heaven Can Wait"?

"Well," you may say, "it sounds fine. I do want to be happy with a lasting kind of happiness.
I do want to get the most out of life.
I want to be successful.
I would like to feel that there is a God who is interested in me and my life.
Of course, I don't want to make any big mistakes that will mar my life—that will mess it all up.

"I would like to believe that it is not simply a lot of senti-mental pious nonsense to say that God cares whom I marry ...
        that marriages are still made in heaven
        that somewhere there is a particular person for me
    that I can feel close to God in my daily life
but—let's be practical.

"Suppose I am ready to call your bluff!
Suppose I am willing to give it a trial.
How does God become real to me?
What do I do?"

These are legitimate questions—if asked by an open mind.
All right, let's be specific ...
If you want anything in this life, you must reach out for it,
                    the right job ...
                the ideal marriage partner ...
            achievement in any area.

Just so, if you desire the treasures in the Christian life, they will not come to you unless you seek them.

Christ said, "And all things, whatsoever ye shall ask in prayer, believing ye shall receive."

Notice that the *ask*—which is action on your part—has to come first of all.

He also said:

> "Ask, and it shall be given you;
> seek, and ye shall find;
> knock, and it shall be opened unto you."   *Matthew 7:7*

The key words here are action words: *ask . . .*
seek . . .
knock.

Jesus never said that there was plenty of time.

He never said to take it easy now and things would work out.

He never suggested that you can sow your oats while young,
because there will always be a chance later on
to straighten out your life.

He never told us "Heaven will wait while you make up your mind about Me."

Jesus Himself was a Man of action.

He did not want publicity
praise
comforts
success as the world measures it . . .

He wanted lives—all or nothing.

He has never changed.

He wants your life committed to Him
now—not tomorrow.

And you would be surprised at the wonderful changes that can come into the life of anyone who is willing to say to Jesus Christ:
> "Yes, I do want to give myself to You today. Here I am. Please take over the direction of my life in every area."

That was the case back in the eighteenth century in the life of the British parliamentarian, William Wilberforce.
I first learned of him in my history textbooks in Scotland.

As a teen-ager, Wilberforce had idled through Pocklington School, and then through St. John's College, Cambridge.
After that, he had spent several years enjoying London's society life.
Later he was to comment that he "could not look back without unfeigned remorse" on all the opportunities he had neglected during those years in school.

Then in 1784, he went to Nice, France, with an old friend, Isaac Milner. During the trip, Milner talked seriously to Wilberforce about what he was going to do with his life . . .
> Was he going to drift with the tide of London society?
> What did he intend to do about the talents God had given him?

The result of this talk was that before he got back to England, William Wilberforce did hand his life
> his dreams
> his future
> his potential over to God.

Changes in the young man's life came thick and fast.
Within three years he knew that God had given him a special assignment . . .

It was a prodigious one, breathtaking:
He was to end forever the vicious slave trade of the then far-
flung British Empire.

How could one man achieve that?
The slave trade cut directly across some of the most powerful
financial interests of the Empire.
Wilberforce knew that since God had given him the assign-
ment, God was in the fight too.
So this young man rolled up his sleeves and soon became a
voice to reckon with in Parliament.
His days of drifting were over.
>   Now his life had a goal.
>   He was on God's side.
And he found within himself unflagging zeal for a fight on
those terms.

The fight took forty-six years in all, but God and Wilberforce
won it.
By act of Parliament, the British emancipated every slave in
the Empire twenty-two years before we achieved the same end
in this country with the bloodshed of the War Between the
States.

Do changes take place in a life handed over to God? Yes, al-
ways . . .
Adventure? Decidedly . . .
Does a goal emerge and with it an understanding of that goal?
Yes. But it begins for each of us with an act of commitment.

I knew a girl named Jane who came to Washington from a
small town in the Midwest.
She was excited about her nation's capital . . .

stirred by the monuments to greatness she saw . . .
awed by the famous names.

She was a wholesome girl—the type you would like to have
for a daughter
    or a sister
      or a friend.
She dreamed of serving her country, of filling a need.
Her story is, in a way, the story of all quiet lonely girls in a new
city.

Jane became a typist in an office with many girls, in a govern-
ment office on Constitution Avenue.
She soon discovered that one can be lonely in the midst of
many.
A shy girl can get lost in a big city . . .
A girl with ideals may not immediately attract men.
Jane became a steady worker, reliable, conscientious.
In a simple, wholesome way she was attractive, and she did
receive invitations to a few parties.

At first she accepted these invitations eagerly.
But when she saw what went on, she felt sick inside . . .
              the constant drinking
            the petty gossip
         the blatant sexuality
        the lack of sincerity.
It was hard to refuse invitations, because she needed friends.
Yet she felt soiled and unclean when she came home.

There were times when the pressure of it all made her wonder
why she held on to her ideals, when other people seemed to
be having a good time without scruples.
    without being bothered by ideals.

After some of these parties, Jane made concessions, compromised with her conscience.
It seemed the thing to do.
Yet the memories of what happened made her blush and feel miserable.

She knew she could never be happy that way—not really happy.
But Jane was puzzled, because neither was she happy as she was now—in her loneliness.

Then came a sudden new temptation, worse than the others because it devastated her at the center of her greatest need— her loneliness.
She was torn, seared by the desire to do something she knew was completely wrong.

All that she believed, all her ideals stood in her path.
She longed to thrust them ruthlessly aside, to say "Yes" to a young man's proposition.
He liked her; she liked him. Why not?
                              Heaven can wait!

Jane went to her room to think it over.
There the four cold walls of the drab one-room apartment,
                the comfortless furniture,
            her aloneness and confusion overwhelmed her.

She buried her head in her hands, sobbing "Oh God—
        Why am I so miserable? Oh God—help me!"
And although she heard nothing, something made her look up.
        Jesus was there by her side.

Jane was startled, but she did not feel fear.
Something about His Presence calmed her,
                    dried her tears:
                His compassionate face . . .
            understanding eyes . . .

It was His eyes that seemed to phrase the statement:
"You called for Me!"

How universal the appeal—man loses the way and cries for his Maker.
He comes in many ways . . .
Through the gentle illumination of a thought . . .
In the soothing coolness of understanding that dissolves hot emotion . . .
In the brilliance of light that pierces foul darkness.
And He comes also as a Presence—a living Presence.

Jane found herself pouring out to Him all her unhappiness . . .
Her disappointments
Her loneliness
Her fears
Her temptation.
She was ashamed as she spoke, but the look of love never left His eyes.
And suddenly she realized that Jesus already knew everything about her.
But that had not changed His love.

Finally Jane phrased the question: "Why am I so unhappy?"
Quietly came the answer: "He who loseth himself for my sake will find himself. Follow thou Me."
And then with a smile of amazing tenderness, He said:
"Lo, I will be with you always."

And then suddenly He was gone.
Yet there was still that strange and wonderful warmth in the room.
The furniture did not seem so drab . . .
Something was different inside her too . . .

> She felt new hope . . .
>> new determination to stand on principle . . .
>> an inner buoyancy, a zest for life . . .
>> and a new love for the girls whom she had envied and
>> even despised.

But most wonderful of all, she knew that never again could she doubt that Jesus cared about her—even her.

There is a place in the heart of God for you too . . .
It is reserved in your name.
Is it empty still?
Then it is empty only because you have not claimed it.

When you do, you will be home.
You will know for yourself His warm and wonderful love,
>> how He will guide you,
>> and help you,
>> give you joy you have never had before.

Isn't it worth trying?
> Heaven can wait?
Ah, but when we can have the joy of Heaven now—
> who wants to wait?

·III·

◄§ Jean had heard from some of her friends that Peter Marshall was preaching at the Montreat, North Carolina, conference grounds that Sunday night. She had paid no particular attention because in her sixteen-year-old eyes, every preacher was like every other preacher.

But that evening found Jean with nothing more exciting to do, so she wandered into the great auditorium and dropped down in a back seat. What happened after that Jean later put down in a theme the following year at school . . .[1]

"As soon as the speakers mounted the platform, I thought I recognized Peter Marshall. The big, burly Scotsman must be he. . . . Yet that was the man I had seen wrestling with some young boys on the lawn outside the auditorium. Plainly he showed the effects of the wrestling: his Palm Beach suit was wilted and his curly hair untidy.

"After Dr. Marshall had been introduced, he rose and walked slowly to the pulpit. This was the same man I had seen outside—yet different. Then he had been like an overgrown boy, handling as many as two or three youngsters at a time, laughing boisterously as he threw them.

"Now he was a man—strong, earnest. There was something about a smile that played over his face that suggested that he had been communing with an unseen Power and had gotten some special light on the task before him.

"He stood there in no hurry to begin, his big hands resting on the open Bible, looking into the faces of the people. He *seemed to be reading their individual needs. Then slowly and clearly he began to speak in his deep, yet musical voice.*

"*After the first few sentences, I edged out of my seat and crept much further front. Dr. Marshall's voice had carried perfectly to the back of the auditorium, but I did not want to miss the least change of expression on his face or the slightest motion.*

"*The sermon built in tempo. Certainly I had heard a lot about Jesus all my life. But Peter Marshall was introducing me to a Christ I had never met before. His voice grew vibrant with feeling. Sometimes to emphasize a point, one huge fist would come crashing down on the pulpit. From time to time he would mop his forehead with a crushed handkerchief and push an unruly lock of damp hair out of his eyes.*

"*For over an hour I sat spellbound, not moving, forgetting all about time. Then suddenly Dr. Marshall was finished. There was no tapering off, no 'And now in conclusion—' He just sat down. There was almost an audible sigh from the crowd, then a hush. . . .*

"*The benediction was pronounced. Few people spoke as they left; no one seemed to want to break the spell.*

"*I slipped out the rear door, hurried back to our cottage, and crawled into bed without a word to anyone. I wanted only one thing: to sense to the fullest—right then—the companionship of that Christ who was so real to Peter Marshall.*"

The sermon Jean heard that evening was "The Chains of Freedom."

THE CHAINS OF FREEDOM

THE great yearning of youth is for freedom.
To be free ... to be on your own ...
    to be your own master.
Does not your blood tingle at the thought of it?

But wait a minute—
If you had the freedom to go where you wanted ...
If you had the money, and your parents would not stop you ...
and you could take off tomorrow ...
Where would you go?
What would you do?

This was exactly the situation confronting a young man whose
story I once heard ...
Robert Duvois wanted his freedom.
He did not like the slow tempo of country life, even though
"Twin Oaks" was a large plantation in South Carolina.

He thought his older brother stuffy.
His father, while kind and sympathetic enough, had some old-
fashioned ideas.
Only his mother might have understood, but she had died six
months before his twenty-first birthday.
I have no freedom here, Robert kept telling himself.
Life seemed a cramped sort of thing,
    always in the same old groove,
        no excitement.

John, the elder son, had inherited his father's business ability and steadfast character.
Gradually his father had let John take over the management of the plantation.

Robert had his mother's artistic, restless temperament.
He wanted to go to Paris to study art.
He wanted to be free to paint—to live, really live.

Finally he could stand it no longer.
"Give me," he said to his father as he sought to get his hands on his inheritance.
"Give me," he said to life, as his young blood tingled with anticipation.
"Give me," he said to the world, and his eyes danced with the excitement of it.

There were entrancing worlds and fascinating people beyond the discipline of home.
He was of age now, old enough to live his own life.
He had money coming from his mother's estate.
"A man has to do what he has to do," he told his father.

The father recognized that he could no longer hold his younger son at home.
He would merely chafe, grow resentful, and eventually leave anyway.

So the father turned over the inheritance to his son.
Some of the money was sent to a Paris bank.
And Robert had his freedom . . .
　　　He was twenty-one . . .
　　　　　with enough money to be his own boss.
What more could anyone ask?

At first, all went well in Paris.
Robert took his art studies seriously.

He wrote his father that several of his oils had been hung in art exhibits.
Then, gradually, the gay life of the French capital began to lure him.
He moved to a fine apartment, bought a sports car.

As he experimented with life, soon on all sides he found himself faced with restrictions to his freedom.
For example, as he drove his car along the Rue de Rivoli he was halted by stop signs and red lights.
Even with Robert's tendency toward self-pity, he knew that the traffic lights were impersonal
                    unfeeling
                    playing no favorites.

He was free to drive through a red light . . .
        but he was not free to avoid the subsequent collision.
He was free to eat whatever he liked in his favorite Paris restaurants, but if he ate too much of exotic foods in combination, he was not free of the gastronomical consequences.

In the realm of his art, his freedom was limited by his ability or lack of it.
He would see wraithlike mists rising from the Seine . . .
        gay colors of sidewalk cafés under their awnings,
                cypresses bathed in shimmering light . . .
but he was not free to capture on canvas what he saw because there was a limit to his talent.

He was free, free to be a traditionalist
                or an impressionist
                or to turn to Cubism or Surrealism . . .
yet whatever art he chose was held in bondage by his own limitations.

In order to overcome these limitations, he would have to sit
at the feet of those who knew more than he did,
    study techniques,
        paint . . . paint . . . paint, hundreds of hours.
It was easier to neglect his studies for the theater,
                gay parties,
                    night life in the cafés.
There was a procession of women upon whom Robert lavished
gifts
    jewels
        furs and perfume.
"Monsieur Robert" 's name soon became well known, even in
Paris, for wealth and extravagance and dissipation.
At last he felt really free.

This was the life, he thought.
And the "substance" which represented years of hard work,
              of sacrifice
              and saving on the part of his parents
was scattered to gratify passing whims, to try to satisfy greedy
desires that were fed but never fulfilled.

One morning, the young man woke to the bitter realization
that his money was gone.
He was in debt to his clothier
           his landlord
        his clubs
        his jeweler.
All his creditors were hounding him.

Hurriedly he left Paris for a small town in Normandy.
There he lived for a few months—guiltily—at a small country
inn where he tried to go back to his painting.
But the joy and inspiration had gone out of it.

Besides, he scarcely had enough money even for paint supplies.

Finally his past caught up with him.
All his possessions, even his clothes, were confiscated.
There was nothing for him to do but to seek work with one of
the local farmers.

At first, he was made an overseer for a wealthy landowner, but
he had little business ability, and what he had was drowned in
the unquenchable thirst for drink to which he was now a slave.
Years passed.
He had long since lost touch with his home.
Things went from bad to worse, until finally he ended up a
hired hand, herding the sheep and tending the pigs.
The vestiges of the sensitive, artistic nature that had once been
his recoiled from every sight and smell of the barnyard and the
pigsty.
He loathed his surroundings,
        his work
and most of all—himself.

Then somehow the boy came to himself.
Memories of home came surging back before the jaded and
bloodshot eyes of the playboy turned ragged swineherd.
Something—the wooing of God's spirit in his heart,
        the early training of his father and mother,
            the inherent quality of the boy's nature—
something brought him back to himself.

He thought of "Twin Oaks" and the gracious, orderly life he
had left behind.
Wistfully he compared his days with those of the workers on
his father's plantation.
Nostalgically he remembered Christmas back home.
The roast turkey with chestnut stuffing . . .

the platters of fried chicken
the beaten biscuits
watermelon-rind preserves
pecan pies
spoon bread
and cold floating island.

He remembered the look in his father's eyes as he had stood
at the head of the table carving the turkey,
the look of tender pride as he had surveyed his family.

Once again he could feel his father's strong arms around
him . . .
a big hand laid tenderly on a little boy's head that day his
puppy had been killed.
Dimly he recalled certain moments of growing up when he
had thought his father stuffy, old-fashioned.
Now everything in him cried out for some of that old-fashioned
love.

That night he crept away from the farm, and on foot made his
way to Cherbourg, where he worked his way back across the
Atlantic on a freighter.
He was going home . . .

Yes, the story does have a familiar ring. You have heard it
before.
It is the old, old story of the Prodigal Son,
as old as man's sin,
as new as God's forgiveness for every man who thinks that
freedom means the license to do what he pleases.

All of us have to begin by discovering what freedom is . . .
and what it is not.
The first valuable revelation is that freedom is not rebellion,
not anarchy.

Sometimes the act of rebelling . . .
  throwing off parental restraints,
   flouting accepted conventions of society,
    renouncing old and accepted beliefs,
gives the exciting illusion of freedom.

Thus every country and every generation has its equivalent of
the Latin quarter,
   its Montmartre,
  its Shepherds' Market,
  or its Greenwich Village,
and the hot-blooded radicals who live there.

The problem is that a man cannot live negatively,
  just in terms of what he is *against*.
   The more pertinent question is,
    what is he *for*?
Once all parental restraints are withdrawn, then what?
Around what will the "free" one build his life?

Many of the moralities and proprieties against which the
younger generation of the Roaring Twenties revolted and
against which the young writers and painters crusaded seem
trifling now.
Today as then, the trouble with the nonsense verse and the
abstract paintings which flow out of these apostate hearts is
that once you subtract the rebellion—
  no matter how artfully expressed—
you have little or nothing left.

The same mistake of confusing anarchy with freedom is made
over and over by political or racial groups struggling to cast off
shackles.
See the Marquis de La Fayette standing on the balcony of the
Château of Versailles beside Louis XVI and Marie Antoinette

pleading ... pleading with his rioting fellow countrymen not to fall into this trap.

But they would not heed; La Fayette could not stem the tide.
   The heady wine of anarchy was already brewed.
So blood flowed in rivers down the gutters of the Place de la Concorde from La Guillotine.
Liberté ... Égalité ... Fraternité ...

Ah, but in the end, murder,
                    drunken mobs with heads on pikes,
                    lawlessness,
                         frenzied promiscuity,
                         anarchy
turned out to be not freedom—but chaos.

Of course you can see it in such extreme instances.
But in the ordinary course of our lives, each of us has to find for himself that there is more to this freedom than rebellion.

It is also true that freedom is not planlessness.
I am reminded of the child in kindergarten who grew tired of having the play period planned and supervised.
He rebelled at having to play group games.

So the teacher finally told him to find his own amusement,
                    do whatever he wanted to do.
It was not long before the rebel was back, grumbling,
"What can I do now? I don't want to do what I want to do."

On a more adult level, a recent spokesman of the school of self-expression and self-indulgence made the same confession: "We took what we wanted, and now we find we no longer want what we took."
There you have the disillusionment that inevitably follows liberty without restraint or plan.

In genuine freedom the plan comes from inside a man.
In the case of Robert Duvois—given his time to use it as he
chose—what did he choose to do?

He was on the right track, so long as he was attempting to
express his true inner self through his painting.
But as soon as this trailed off into irresponsibility . . .
"wasting his substance in riotous living . . ."
then this young man had betrayed freedom.

The more irresponsible he became, the less freedom he had,
the more hemmed in he was by poverty,
the more he was shackled by the tyranny of habits,
the more he was confined by the laws of man and God
that play no favorites and will step aside for no one.

And then—at a crisis moment—Robert Duvois turned himself
around to take his first good look at what freedom really is.
True freedom is finding oneself . . . choosing oneself.
Always in that process, one or more false concepts of what
he *thought* he was must die.
That is why Jesus' "For whosoever will save his life shall lose
it . . ." is found today to be an incisively penetrating psycho-
logical insight.

Then, once the self is found, for the first time man accepts
full responsibility for that self . . .
for the choices he makes,
the disciplines he imposes upon himself,
the way he relates to other human beings.

No longer does he interpret freedom as rebellion against
realities.
Now he accepts himself, other people, and circumstances *as
they are* and uses his freedom to shape his circumstances
creatively.

At this point he discovers the paradox at the heart of all truth:
We want our freedom in order to give our love and our
loyalty away to something bigger than ourselves.

Michelangelo wanted to be an artist, but his father objected.
He wanted no son of his to be "a stonecutter."
But the passion to create was in Michelangelo's blood, so at age
thirteen—over his father's stubborn opposition—the boy left
home.
He was free now...Yet what a bondservant to art Michelan-
gelo became!
Long hours of work...
pinching hardship...
superhuman labor...
Two years, three months of grueling toil to complete the statue
"David"...
Over four and a half years to paint the ceiling vault of the
Sistine Chapel...
Free—yet voluntarily bound.

We can watch the same pattern with many a scientist.
See Marie Curie in her laboratory—her fine mind,
all her training in physics,
every moment she could spare, day or night,
utter devotion
given to refining from pitchblende a new substance—radium.

In the end, Marie Curie laid down her life on the altar of
science because, during those long days and nights of work, she
had been exposed to radium too often.
A free woman, but she had given her love and her loyalty away.
Yet we can never doubt that this is real freedom, because it is
the heart's voluntary loyalty,
the man's or the woman's own choice.

Long centuries before, God's first direct word on behalf of His
chosen people had been the thundering "Let my people go," to
the pharaoh who held them in bondage.
After that, through the long years of Israel's history
    through wanderings and captivities
      through times of obedience and
        through times of falling away—
God's word never changed—"Let my people go."

Finally, the word came to Jesus.
It is no accident that Jesus Christ is so concerned with freedom.
That day in Nazareth when He stood in the local synagogue to
announce His Messiahship to His astounded relatives and
friends, a major portion of the platform of His Kingdom was
    "deliverance to the captives."

Then He proceeded to live this out episode by episode ...
    He freed many a one bound by sin.
      Everywhere He went, He released the captives of pain
      and disease.
        With gladness, He threw open the dark dun-
        geons of hate to the sunlight of God's love.
          He struck the shackles from tortured minds
          and personality compulsions.
Moreover He went on to more dangerous liberties:
He declared war on the bondage of ossified traditions
               and man-made dogmas.
Almost every point of the Sermon on the Mount begins with
"It hath been said of them of old time. ..."
    "But I say unto you. ..."
Tangling with entrenched religious tradition ...
Dangerous! Of course it was dangerous!

Yet if you read the accounts of Christ for yourself, you will see
that He had no trace of fear of public opinion.
Physical fear seems to have been unknown to Him:
He never hesitated to touch any loathsome leper . . .
On more than one occasion He walked through the
midst of a rioting mob . . .
He slept through a violent storm on the Sea of
Galilee . . .
He faced spies and inquisitors, temple au-
thorities, King Herod, or Pontius Pilate
with an equanimity nothing could shake.

"Fear not them which kill the body," He advised His disciples.
His words were prophetic.
Finally, His was the supreme freedom:
He was free even to go to His Cross.

This point He made over and over, so that no man could mis-
take it:
"I lay down My life. . . .
No man taketh it from Me.
I have power to lay it down,
and I have power to take it again."
John 10:17, 18

Yes, Christ was the freest Man who ever lived.
Yet—here is the paradox again—He was free because He had
given His love and His loyalty away.
Voluntarily, He had made His Father's will supreme:

"I seek not mine own will," He said repeatedly,
"but the will of the Father which hath sent me."
John 5:30

Out of such freedom and such loyalty always comes intense
joy.

Just here, we do violence to the New Testament narratives if we imagine Christ to be a melancholy recluse.
Isaiah prophesied that He would be "a man of sorrows and acquainted with grief."
Yes, but that was in order that *our* joy might be full.
A Christ who with trembling lower lip and tear-filled eyes looked wistfully at human joy is a caricature that belies the records.

On the contrary, the picture of Jesus in the Gospels is of a radiant, laughter-loving Friend whom everybody loved, save the cynical . . . the hard . . . the hating, who had lost the art of loving anybody.

He was a guest at the wedding feast at Cana because He enjoyed human fun and fellowship.
He was criticized because of the company He kept . . .
    sneeringly referred to as "a friend of publicans and sinners . . ."
    even called "a winebibber."

The humble folk heard Him gladly, indeed idolized Him.
Children flocked to Him eagerly, and children never go to the austere, stern person sunk in perpetual gloom.

Always Christ's message is that His Father has designed you and me for freedom and for happiness.
Having counted the world *joy* 191 times in the Scriptures . . .
glad or *gladness* 125 times, at that point I gave up counting.

God is a God of laughter as well as of prayer . . .
    a God of singing as well as of tears.
God is at home in the play of His children . . .
    He loves to hear us laugh.

Every one of Jesus' beatitudes begins with the words
  blessed or *happy*.
He came to give you the secrets of living, He said,
  so that "your joy might be full."

"Your joy no man taketh from you," He insists.   *John 16:22*
Indeed, so much does He cherish our liberty and our joy that
if we will let Him—He will see to it that no one takes it from
us.
He will stand shoulder to shoulder beside us
  and battle for our freedom.
This is the point at which turning to Him can be dangerous
business.
For when we get right down to it, most of us *like* some of
our shackles,
  feel so comfortably secure in some of our prisons that we
  resist final maturity and ultimate responsibility.
But Christ will tolerate no compromise with our liberty.

The tyranny of lust or greed cannot abide His presence.
  The despotism of jealousy flees before Him.
    Always He opens the door to the dungeon of judging.
    He can heal the bindings of painful memories and
    bitter remorse.
      He sets Himself against the dictatorship of stand-
      ardization and social conformity.
        He had specific words to speak against parental
        or family domination.

Now will you listen to Christ when He says:
  "The Spirit of the Lord is upon Me because . . .
    He hath sent Me to . . . preach deliverance to the cap-
    tives"?   *Luke 4:18*
The captives are you and me.

Yet with Christ Himself as our example—we, like Him, have to give our love and our loyalty away.
In the end, there is only One into whose hands we dare entrust the keys to our personal freedom.

Once we put those keys in Christ's hands, we have a surprise awaiting us.
We had feared that giving Him our loyalty would cramp us,
    that He would give us a long list of forbidden pleasures.

That is not His way.
"Where the Spirit of the Lord is, there is liberty," the apostle Paul exults.   *II Corinthians* 3:17

All during his ministry, Paul battled "the false brethren who come to spy out our liberty in Christ Jesus" by setting up moral and ritualistic restrictions.

Augustine was right:
Christ's way is "Love God, and do as you please."

As you grow to love God, what you "please" will change.
This is where the surprise comes in.
God gives the inner man a new set of goals and passions.
It would be bondage indeed to obey God when we do not want to; it is delightful freedom to do what we most want to do.
And that is the wonderful way that God works it out for us.

It is at that point that, like Robert Duvois, we come to ourselves, experience for the first time real freedom.
For like Robert Duvois, every one of us has misused the freedom that God gave us.
The story of the Prodigal Son is the story of every man.

And when the sands of the desert grow cold . . .
    when the stars go out one by one . . .
        when the earth is rolled up like a carpet . . .

and thrown over the high balconies of heaven . . .

 when our clever sciences have been forgotten . . .
when the proud boasts of men have been carried away on the
hurricanes of time,

 this story will still speak to us . . .
Of a boy who lost his way
Of a Father who freely forgave him.

It will still have the power to soften our hard hearts and bring
tears to our eyes.
It will still point the way to the heart's true home,

 still unfold to us the love of God.
For this story that Jesus told contains the most appealing pic-
ture of God ever drawn.
This parable contains the heart of the gospel:

 That God is willing, indeed eager, to forgive
 sinners like you and me,

 that the moment we turn around to take the way back
 home, the Father will come running down the road to
 meet us . . .
That He is the One who alone holds in His hands the keys to
our freedom.

 "Make me a captive, Lord,
 And then I shall be free;
 Force me to render up my sword;
 And I shall conqueror be. . . ."

·IV·

&§ One of Peter Marshall's favorite sermon illustrations—
especially in the early years of his ministry—was "the King is
in the audience." It was a vivid word picture of a scene typical
of the London theater.

He described the waiting audience filing slowly into seats
that tipped down with a welcoming clatter.... The cheerful
conversation that spread from row to row and spilled into the
foyer. He spoke of the orchestra, emerging stooping, tuning its
instruments; of the scenes backstage—ropes, cables, hoisting
gear being tried out.... Lights being focused and shutters
placed in readiness.

In the dressing room each mirror framed a face being
made up. Finally warning lights winked backstage. Silence ...
places.... The overture had begun. But in the middle, a phrase
was broken off; the orchestra stopped abruptly. There was a
moment of deathly stillness—then the stately, thrilling strains
of the National Anthem.

In the wings, the stage manager and director ran excitedly
from group to group, "Give it all you've got tonight. Play as
you've never played before."

Why? Why this commotion? Because ... The King is in
the audience.

For Peter Marshall it was a parable of human life. Often
he would tell his congregations, "The King is in this audience
—walking these aisles or sitting beside you. You may whisper

your prayer to the King now"—and heart-searching silence would follow. You seemed to feel Him there in the quiet sanctuary, to hear the rustling of His robe.

But Peter's message was that the King is not in the audience just for one night, that the King is not confined to the church. He is in His world, all of His world, in the joy of it and also in the heartbreak. He is in the laughter of children, but also with the old people left without affection; in the healthy fun of youth, but also with the wives lonely at home. The King is standing beside the bride with shining eyes, but He is also suffering with the woman on the sickbed or with the men who must live beneath the thunder of the guns and the whine of the shells.

Peter knew that his unique mission in life was to introduce men and women to the King walking among them, to make men aware of Him. Who is the King? Even this Jesus.

The plaque in the foyer of the new building for the New York Avenue Presbyterian Church in Washington bears this inscription:

TO PETER MARSHALL

WHO MADE JESUS CHRIST A LIVING REALITY

TO THE CONGREGATION OF NEW YORK AVENUE.

JOHN DOE, DISCIPLE

THERE are many of you who think of Christ as someone who belongs to history—like Caesar

or Washington,
or Napoleon.
You think of Him as one who lived on earth and passed away.
A great man, to be sure, but nothing more.

Perhaps you look on His life as an affecting sacrifice,
                                    a great inspiration.
He was a Wise Teacher, you say, but beyond that Christ is not
really significant for you.

Or do you have an inner contempt for the mild, suffering Jesus
so often pictured?
It is a curious thing that the artists whose brushes have traced
His form on canvas have largely portrayed His gentleness,
                                    meekness
                                    compassion
                                    suffering . . .
rather than the other, equally true sides of His personality . . .
                                    strength
                                    tireless energy
                                    uncompromising will.

Perhaps it is this one-sided picture of the meek and longsuffer-
ing Christ that you and I *want* to see.
Perhaps it is the picture that more nearly suits our generation
with its broad-mindedness
        its easygoing compromises
            its scorn of hell
                its denial of the reality of sin.

But when we throw away our preconceived ideas and turn to
the New Testament for ourselves, we come away with an altogether different conception.

There is a true picture of Christ in the Gospel of John—
a dramatic scene in the Temple of Jerusalem near the beginning of Jesus' public ministry.
It is His first appearance before His nation as the Messiah.

No one could forget it . . . Jesus walking through the colonnade
with its marble forest of great Corinthian pillars a hundred
feet high, then on into the Court of the Gentiles.

It is early morning, but already the temple court is a bedlam of
activity and noise.
Among the tables of the moneychangers, the cages of doves
and the stalls of cattle, people crowd about
        chatting with their friends,
        selecting a dove for sacrifice,
or getting their money from Tyre or Persia or Egypt or Geece
changed into the sacred half-shekel of the sanctuary.
It is convenient to buy sacrifices on the spot instead of having
to drag them from a distance.
It is helpful to be able to exchange money bearing upon it the
head of the emperor, a graven image and therefore unaccept-
able in the Temple, for the statutory half-shekel.

And so, convenient for all and profitable to many, the temple
huckstering has become a recognized institution.
Shrill voices bargaining
    swearing angrily
      bickering
the metallic tinkle of coins as they drop into the moneyboxes
on the table . . .
all the signs of greed can be heard just outside the Holy Place.
There is no serenity—no peace.
No one can pray there.

Suddenly there is a lull in the confusion.
Startled at the sudden quiet, we look up to find a strange yet
hauntingly familiar figure standing between two of the gigantic
stone columns, His eyes burning with intensity,
             His face magnificent in its wrath.
Poor peasants are being bled in the name of God.
Has He not watched His own mother patching clothes,
                       skimping on food
to save one denarius after another for the Temple dues?

As He steps forward with a resolution and firmness born of
the terrible conviction that shines in His face, there is a look
in His eyes before which men break away.
His lips are drawn into a thin line . . .

Stooping, He picks up some binding cords which the merchants
have discarded.
Deftly He knots them into a whip.

There is something in His attitude,
                 in His eyes,
                 in His face,
in that ominous silence in which He stands watching,
which makes men look at Him with uneasiness in their eyes.

And then the full fury of His wrath breaks.
In a few long strides He is across the court.
Picking up the boxes filled with money—scornfully and deliberately—He empties them on the stone floor . . . and the
coins spill with a clatter and go rolling in a hundred directions.

The tables too go crashing to the floor, and the moneychangers
rush to gather up their coins from the filth.
In their greed—made all the more frantic because of their fear

—they grovel in the dirt, pouncing upon their money and screaming in protest as the Man with the whip stands over them.

And then He drives out the terror-stricken cattle.
The muscles of His arms stand out like cords;
    lights dart from His eyes.

Not a voice is heard in protest . . .
    not a hand is raised against Him.
Even the Temple guards only stand and watch helplessly.
His magnificent figure dominates the scene.

His voice rings out, echoing among the stone pillars, and it sounds like the voice of doom . . .
    like the voice of God Himself . . .
"It is written, My house shall be called the house of prayer, but ye have made it a den of thieves."

Who is this Christ?

He is a Man whose impact on people who listened to Him must have been more like dynamite than dew.
One cannot read the Gospels without reaching the conclusion that there was something disturbing about the march of the Galilean through the land.
Everywhere He went there was anything but peace.
    Debates and arguments buzzed around Him.

If men did not come to Him with questions,
He challenged their thinking with questions of His own.
He made men wonder about themselves . . .
look into their hearts and see things they had not seen before.
He made them ponder about life and what it meant.

C 77

Who is this Christ?

In talking to young people I have the feeling that there is
confusion about Jesus ...
To many, He is a dim shadowy figure ... almost a stranger.

You have heard echoes of His person ...
    rumors of His movements in the hearts and lives of people
    around you.
But again and again you have missed Him—as though He were
some romantic figure moving about the pitched tents of an
army at night.
You have heard stories of Him whispered around the campfires
before which young people seek to warm their souls.

Yet, always you miss Him and grow weary in the search
until you question in your heart His mysterious person.
The fact is that you really have not met Him face to face.
An introduction may help.
John Doe, I would like you to meet One who means everything
to me ...
John Doe, meet Jesus of Nazareth.

This Christ—whence did He come?
His home was in an obscure village of an occupied Roman
province.
He was born in a stable where animals from the inn were kept.
His parents were poor working people.
The only records we have of Him are silent about the greater
part of His life.
This remains one of the most intriguing historical mysteries of
all time.

There are hints that after Joseph's death He took over the
family carpentry shop—first in Nazareth, then in Capernaum.

His formal education was in the local synagogue school, and
it stopped when He was twelve.
He left no writings.
Indeed, the only record of His having written anything is one
of finger tracings in the sand ... and the eddies of wind that
swirled around the pillars of the Temple porch soon covered
it up.

He spoke Aramaic, the traditional Hebrew, and probably a
smattering of Greek and Latin, for He lived in a trilingual
world.
Never did He travel more than a hundred miles from home.
Standing on the Mount of Olives He could look over the
length and breadth of His country ... which He never left
during His life.

When He began His public ministry and took to preaching,
His family tried to talk Him out of it, thinking and saying that
He was mad.

His friends were mostly as poor as He was—fisherman and
peasants.
See Him mingling with the forgotten men,
        talking to the outcasts,
      knowing no social barriers,
    caring nothing for money or material things,
  going about with publicans and sinners
until many of His contemporaries were scandalized.

He attracted great crowds, for He walked among the sick,
                        touching here a blind eye,

there a palsied limb,
here a running sore,
there a crippled leg.
Even His enemies were later to admit these miracles.

But finally the crowds drifted away, for His counsels were too difficult; men were not ready to accept this hard way of love.
And so the sands ran out and His three-year ministry drew to its close.
At one point, He feared that His own followers might also melt away.
In the end, most of them did flee in fear, caring more for their own safety than for Him.

He died a criminal's death, reviled and mocked . . .
tormented and laughed at,
hanging between two thieves.
They buried Him in a borrowed grave.

But the story was not finished.
Suddenly His disciples, the same men who had run away, came back boldly into the streets of the city which had crucified Christ, proclaiming that He was not dead at all—
He was alive.

The body with the marks of the nails and the spikes had disappeared.
On this everyone was agreed.
There were many attempted explanations, but somehow none was adequate.
All that His enemies had to do to silence forever the rumor of this resurrection was to produce the body—but they could not.

Whatever anyone else in Jerusalem thought, it was obvious that Christ's disciples were convinced beyond any doubt that

their Master was alive.
For they were different—not the same men at all.
They were no longer afraid.
They spoke boldly.
Threats did not intimidate them.

They said fantastic things—that the Living God had once and for all, in a brief life on this earth, given a full and final revelation of Himself in Christ.

In Jesus—God had come!

They said that, within thirty-six hours of Christ's death, the dead body had become alive,
had walked out of the grave,
appeared to many human witnesses—to *them*.

Among the pillars of the Temple porch itself, their ringing assertions echoed and reverberated:

"This Jesus whom ye crucified is risen from
the dead and now demands that every man repent."

As you would suppose, such a message was laughed at.
"These men are drunk" was the first popular verdict.
Then "They must be mad."

The wild story traveled fast ... to Asia Minor ... to Rome.
There was derisive laughter—"Just another superstitious cult."
Was not the world of that day satiated with cults and bizarre man-made religions?

But then this Jesus began to be talked about too much and the Roman Empire tried to stop the story's spreading by force and threats.
"Don't tell these tales again," the disciples were told, "if you value your lives."

But they did not stop.
The threats only made them more eloquent and bold.

Thrown into prison, they made the cell a pulpit and the dungeon a choir.
Stoned, they rose from the dust bleeding and bruised, but with a more convincing testimony.
Lashed with whips, they praised God the more.

Nothing could stop them.
The Romans made human torches of believers to light the arenas on their holidays.
Yet in death, these Christian martyrs made converts to their strange preaching.
Hunted and persecuted,
    thrown to the lions,
        tortured and killed,
still the number of those who made the sign of the Cross grew...
    and grew.
Rome could not stop Jesus.
Her grandeur toppled and fell; Jesus lived on.
What the Empire had regarded as a ripple on the wide sea of polytheism became a tidal wave sweeping over the world.
Incredibly, in A.D. 325 under the Emperor Constantine,
Christianity won official recognition from the Empire which had once vowed to crush every last follower of the Nazarene.

In all of history, has there ever been such an extraordinary sequence of events?
Who is this Jesus?
What is the explanation of His power?

Etched against the skyline of every city,
    carried in the forefront of every human endeavor,
    the Cross on which He died has become a haunting
symbol of a haunting Person.
Christ is an end . . . and a beginning.
All secular history is divided into two great divisions:
                before Christ—after Christ.

In an old document, Celsus—a Roman historian—trying to
explain the strange power of Christianity in his day, wrote:

> "The importance of Christianity is the excessive value it
> places on every human soul."

Jesus insisted that God's interest centered on the individual.
His is the power that sets the prisoners free, in whatever
bondage they languish.
Testimonies are without number.
Changed lives all ascribe the glory to Him.
It is to Him that credit belongs for the newness of life and the
victories that men and women have achieved.

How many are there who will testify to this power?
    The power that saves,
        that forgives,
           that leads and guides through life.
There it is . . . a mystery and a power!

But it is more than the power of an idea or a philosophy; more
than the memory of a good and great Man.
He is a Presence now—even now.
"Lo, I am with you always," He once said—and many of us
have found it true—gloriously true.

Part of the mystery is this: that He lived nineteen centuries
ago, in the faraway little land of Palestine.
He wore Oriental robes and sandals.
Yet His words and His Presence are as real and as relevant as
if He had spoken last night on the radio in English
    from New York or San Francisco.
Even in our days of neon signs and penthouses, of skyscrapers
and fast air travel, He is authoritative, the last word for us.

There is no shortage of evidence that the ethical teaching of
Christ is eternally and everlastingly right.
Our best minds today are willing to admit that a great many
things on which we pinned our hopes have failed us miserably.

Man has supposed that his new heaven and his new earth will
come through materialism . . .
    having two cars for every garage,
        a television set in every living room,
            an electric dishwasher and clothes drier.
Somehow these have not brought about the desired results.

Nor has secularism made life happier or easier.
We are all becoming aware with a sickness of heart that a
civilization whose art ends in surrealism . . .
    whose music ends in discord,
        whose literature ends in the airing of sexual license and
        sexual deviations,
            whose science ends in the power to destroy civiliza-
            tion. . . .
can never satisfy the soul of the world or the hunger of the
human heart.

An assistant of Thomas A. Edison once tried to console the
inventor over the failure to achieve in a series of experiments
what he had set out to find:

"It's too bad," he said, "to do all that work without results."
"Oh," said Mr. Edison, "we have lots of results. We know
seven hundred things that won't work."

By this time we ought to know a good many things that will
not work in our world . . .
You and I have even found out one or two philosophies of our
own that have not brought us peace or happiness.

Still that haunting Figure stands in our midst.
Read the New Testament for yourself and see if this same Jesus
does not step out of the pages to stand beside you
          with His piercing eyes and His quiet vibrant voice—
                              like the voice of God—
"Follow Me," He says. "Follow Me . . ."
"Whom say ye that I am?"

What then are you to reply, John Doe?
Have you answered that question in your own mind?
Has your heart whispered its response?
It is a question you cannot dodge forever.

It is today as it was in His day.
When He walked the trails of Palestine, men tried to be
neutral and found that they could not.
Try as they might to brush Him aside—on whatever pretext,
                              they could not have done with Him.
There has always been a quality about Jesus that was urgent.
It had to be accepted—or rejected.
He forced the issue because of the claims He made for Himself.

Consider those claims . . .
He claimed equality with God . . .

"I and My Father are one."   *John 10:30*
"He that hath seen Me hath seen the Father."   *John 14:9*

He claimed to be the fulfillment of Old Testament prophecy.
He stated that before Abraham was born, He had lived . . .
He said that He had come from God in heaven, and that
He would return to His Father.

Such talk was not misunderstood by the Jews.
Jesus meant that it should be understood, and it was.
Knowing full well the meaning of what He had claimed,
                    they howled for His death . . .

"Therefore the Jews sought the more to kill Him, because
He . . . said also that God was His own Father, making
Himself equal with God."   *John 5:18*

Christ accepted the worship of men.
He took it as His right, accepted it as His prerogative.
When Simon Peter or Thomas or many another worshiped
Him, He did not say, "Stand up on your feet, for I am like
yourselves."
He took their worship and breathed upon them His benediction.

He affirmed His sinlessness.
The challenge He hurled, "Which one of you accuseth Me of
sin?" found none to speak against Him.
It is the testimony of the friends who knew Him best,
        of the enemies who loved Him least.

"I find no fault in this Man," said Pontius Pilate wonderingly.

"This Man hath done nothing amiss," cried the thief dying beside Him.

Christ has been under the microscope for twenty centuries.
Philosophers
    scientists,
       reformers,
          poets and statesmen,
          cynics and saints,
have examined Him for blemishes and found in Him no flaw.

He claimed the right to forgive sin—a prerogative of God.
This was no mechanical formula, no hocus-pocus or black magic, for in every case His pronouncement of pardon was accompanied by a peace of mind and a cleanness of soul that expressed itself in a transformed life,
    a changed outlook,
      a fresh beginning.

He claimed to have the right and the authority to tell men how to get in touch with God.
He told them what to do to find peace and happiness and eternal life.
He gave them new commandments with the authority of God.
He predicted that later He would judge men everywhere.
He claimed to be doing the will of God.

Now as you read the audacious claims made by this Jesus, you are forced to a simple conclusion:
    either the claims are true—or this Man was a charlatan.

If they were false, did He hope to convince people simply by making more stupendous claims than any other human being had ever made?

Men have laughed at fools before . . . have been amused, enter-
tained.
But Christ did not affect them like that.
"Never man spake as this Man," even His enemies admitted.

He placed Himself at the center of His ethic and His message.
He did not come to us to point the way.
He said, "I am the way . . . I am the door . . . I am the truth."

Calmly He obtruded Himself—yet so convincingly that men
were shocked.
Thus Christianity is more than the religion of Jesus:
                                    It is the worship of Christ.

Christ is not only the center; He is also the circumference.
Take Zoroaster out of the religion that bears his name, and
you will still have Zoroastrianism.
Take Mohammed out of Islam, and you will still have the
worshipers of Allah.
But take Jesus Christ out of Christianity, and you have absolutely nothing left.

                    Christianity is Christ.

Now what shall we make of all this?
Either it is sheer nonsense—or it is true.
Either anyone who speaks as Christ did was a mumbling idiot,
        a deranged megalomaniac who thinks that he is a teapot
        . . . or Joan of Arc's horse . . . or Napoleon—
or else Christ was, and is, who He claims to be.

The alternative that He did not leave us is to believe that
He was merely a great moral teacher.
To say this is to betray our ignorance.
For one who made the claims that Christ did—if they were

fraudulent—could scarcely be a great moral teacher.
He would be a maniac, or at the least a consummate liar.

Yet His sanity has never been questioned, for His life and His teachings were too obviously normal and sensible and clear-headed.
In fact, as the relatively new science of psychology is progressively finding out, His teachings of love and selflessness lie at the heart of an integrated personality.

And the suspicion of fraud has no foundation, for the swindlers always use their ability to fool people to gain wealth or power.
Jesus asked nothing.
He taught unselfishness and indifference to the treasures of this world, and His own life is the proof of His sincerity.

Did He then speak the truth?
Was He God come down to earth to show us the loving heart of the Father?
As a matter of fact, there could be no greater proof of the truth of His claims than that I—some nineteen hundred years later—should even be asking the question: "John Doe, what do you think of Christ?"

Perhaps no one has ever confronted you with the fact that what you decide about Him will be the most important decision of your life.

You cannot go on dodging the issue.
You must be either for Him—or against Him.
Even if you try to be noncommittal, that is an answer too.
A man in a burning house to whom the firemen throw a rope ladder may have difficulty deciding whether or not to risk using it.

Should he hesitate too long, he *has* decided.
The notice of his death in next day's newspaper will leave
little doubt of his decision.

What are you going to do with Jesus?

There are stern facts which Christ Himself asks you to consider before you decide.
Few men have ever recruited disciples on such hard-hitting
terms . . .
He warned that following Him might divide families . . .
alienate friends.
He said that it would mean a shift in values,
a turning away from materialism.
It would involve sacrifice, because you would no longer be able
to put yourself and your own comforts first.
For some, hatred, persecution, and death would follow.

Let us not deceive ourselves that these warnings were just for
first-century Christians.
If Christ were to reappear—dressed in a modern business suit
—on Main Street or Madison Avenue, would we react any
differently than did the inhabitants of Jerusalem in A.D. 33?

Would we have enough dedication and stamina
to accept Him and His audacious claims,
to make known our allegiance to Him
under the pressure of an unpopular cause and ostracism?
The sad truth is that purity and sacrifice are unpopular in
every century.

At the moment, we are in a period when church membership
is socially acceptable and on the rise.
It is not hard to decide for Christ so long as He stays safely in
the pages of the New Testament,

or smiles at us on a Sunday morning from a stained-glass window.

But as materialism and secularism accelerate, our civilization may yet, in our time, go full circle.

In that case, we may see a new conspiracy against God,
      a modern version of Christian persecution,
        even of Christianity having to go underground.

These are possibilities you should consider, John Doe.

What then *does* He offer you?

His friendship—the most wonderful friendship in the world.
    His strength for your weakness . . .
      His forgiveness for your sins . . .
        His comfort to your sorrow . . .
          His light to your darkness . . .
            His guidance for your way.

For, start wherever you will in an honest search to find out this truth about this Christ, sooner or later God in Christ will find you.

And then you will have the final, complete proof of His deity—
        in your own experience.

Whenever you look into your own heart, you will find His haunting Presence.

He will show you a love that will never let you go.

"Come after Me," He still calls, asking for recruits,
        for disciples.

Are you ready to answer Him, John Doe?

Are you ready to be—John Doe, Disciple?

·V·

❧ If ever there was a nonconformist, Peter Marshall was one. I remember a night in Miami Beach, for instance, when he was there for a preaching mission. It was late, around midnight, and he was hot and thirsty after his labors. The only places still open were night clubs.

We entered one. There were thick carpets, a hushed atmosphere, and the usual exotic dim lighting. I knew that the latter was one of Peter's pet aversions. "Nothing glamorous about it," he muttered, "just nefarious gloom."

As he followed the maître d', Peter put out his hand like a blind man groping his way. The dignified man in tails looked at us disapprovingly, showed us to a table and then left shaking his head.

In the semidarkness a waiter ceremoniously presented the liquor list. Just as ceremoniously Peter struck a match to look at it. Fighting off laughter, I saw perplexity and indecision flitting across the sedate waiter's face. He looked closely at his customer to see if this one was drunk or joking.

"Ginger ale all right, Catherine?"

I nodded.

"And I want a glass of milk—make it a large glass," Peter said.

The waiter, frustrated by this nonalcoholic order, opened his mouth, shut it again. "Sir, we may not have milk."

"Of course you have milk," Peter answered blithely.

The man stared contemptuously at Peter, trying to intimidate him. Peter stared back unblinkingly. Finally the waiter retreated to fumble in the back of the icebox for some milk.

Peter was enjoying himself hugely. There was nothing he liked better than pricking balloons of pompous conformity. In fact, a look at any area of his life would reveal this same individuality.

His favorites in literature were Shakespeare, Milton, John Buchan, Robert Burns, F. W. Boreham (the Australian), Leslie Weatherhead, George Buttrick, A. A. Milne, and the King James Bible. He had been known to mix any combination thereof in a sermon. Why not? These were men and books he liked.

Clothes? He was fond of the informal—especially open-necked sport shirts. He disliked wearing a hat. Upon appropriate Scottish occasions, he would wear kilts. It was almost impossible to dress him "correctly" for any given occasion.

His tastes in food and drink were an absurd combination of British heritage with American acquisitions: Tea . . . tea . . . tea . . . made properly, of course. Steak-and-kidney pie . . . and corn on the cob. Scottish shortbread . . . angel-food cake. No flavor of ice cream except vanilla in the best British tradition . . . soft boiled custard.

Of course nonconformity in such peripheral areas could have been merely amusing eccentricity. But in Peter's case, he had a way of seeing many accepted conventions with fresh eyes and the courage to act on his personal appraisal.

There was the matter of corporate worship. I saw him hold up his arms to stop a church congregation in the middle of singing a hymn. "Do you really know what you are singing?" he cried.

"I'll go where you want me to go, dear Lord, . . .

Take my silver and my gold.
Not a mite would I withhold. . . .
Do you mean that? I doubt it! Don't sing these words now unless you mean them!"

Race relations? He was ahead of his times. He gloried in the fact that when Chief Justice Charles Evans Hughes was received into the membership of the Calvary Baptist Church in Washington, a Chinese laundress stood beside him, being received at the same time. "The ground at the foot of the Cross is level," he thundered. "Do the words liberty and justice for all mean anything? Where is liberty? . . . If the Spirit of the Living God be not permitted to operate in American hearts to solve the complicated . . . delicate . . . dangerous question of race relationships in this land of ours, then the stone god of paganism will force upon us a solution that will crush and kill every decent thing."

To his prayers in the United States Senate Peter Marshall brought his fresh approach. He refused to use words to lull the Senators to sleep, so many of his prayers were less than one hundred words. There is nothing soporific about challenges like these: "If there be any here sulking as children" or "Take away the stubborn pride that keeps us from apology." He spoke of stomach ulcers as the "badge of lack of faith"; of "swelled heads and stubborn wills"; "Help us to keep our moral voting record straight."

The sermon that follows—"Get Out Of Step"—reflects Peter Marshall's basic belief in the fresh approaches and the creative nonconformity that the Spirit of God can introduce into our lives whenever we let Him.

GET OUT OF STEP

ONE of the memorable scenes in an English novel of some years ago [2] describes how a little boy named Bron goes to church for the first time with his governess.

He watches with interest every part of the service and then the preacher climbs into the high pulpit and Bron hears him give out a piece of terrible news.

It is about a brave and kind man who was nailed to a cross . . . ferociously hurt a long time ago . . . who feels a dreadful pain even now, because there was something not done that He wants them all to do.

Little Bron thinks that the preacher is telling the story because a lot of people are there and they will do something about it.

Bron is sitting impatiently on the edge of the pew.
He can scarcely wait to see what the first move will be in righting this injustice.
But he sits quietly and decides that after the service someone will do something about it.

Little Bron weeps . . . but nobody else seems at all upset.
The service is over, the people walk away as if they had not heard such terrible news,
    as if nothing remarkable had happened.

As Bron leaves the church, he is trembling.
His governess looks at him and says:

"Bron, don't take it to heart—someone will think you are
queer."

Queer—to be alive and sensitive in one's spirit!
Queer—to show emotion!
Queer—to listen to what is going on in God's house,
                                really to hear,
                            to respond . . .
Queer—to take Jesus Christ seriously!

What does *queer* mean?
The dictionary says "differing in some odd way from what is
ordinary."

Ought not the Christian, then, to be queer?
He should not be satisfied with the ordinary in life.
Christ was not ordinary, and He did not call His followers to
be ordinary.

Yet so many people who call themselves Christians today are
living ordinary lives.
There is nothing about them that makes them any different
from others who make no profession of belief, acknowledge
no faith, and assume no obligations.
In fact, like Bron's governess, what they fear most in life is
being "different."
We are becoming an assembly-line society.
The days of rugged individualism that explored the American
frontier have been left far behind.

While this pattern of conformity can be seen in every age
group, I want to speak about it especially to you young people,
because as you huddle together—
        each of you trying to be like everyone else—

you are not finding the satisfactions you seek.

You are still hungry and thirsty on the inside, you still have problems unsolved, questions unanswered.
I want to tell you where you can find some of the answers you seek.

With many of you, conformity has become a creed.
You are terrified at being set apart.
Your own teen-age definition of sin is to be out of step with your friends.

You must wear clothes like everyone else . . .
    collect and listen to the same records
      learn the same dances
        know the latest teen-age slang.

The desire to look and act like everyone else affects all of life:
            your study habits,
           your dating patterns,
        how you spend your time,
       what you buy with your allowance,
your attitude toward parents . . . your nation . . . God . . . the church.

In order not to be different, you have to be content with a low standard of achievement . . .
    a conformity to mediocrity rather than a desire to excel.

Are you, for example, content with average grades, because to excel would be to be thought "a grind"
           "a square"
         just plain queer?

Why read for yourself and draw your own conclusions when it is far safer to adopt the philosophy of your friends,

or favorite columnist,
or television commentator?
The editorial page of our newspaper is ignored by too many
readers who turn to the sports page or the comic strips for
their reading, because they do not wish to do any serious
thinking.

The teen years are the years for discovering "the real you,"
the time when you should be shaping your own tastes.
Yet the temptation with all thoughts, activities, and goals is
to keep right in step,
marching along like robots,
fearful of ridicule . . . criticism . . . isolation . . .
if you should, perchance, get out of step with the crowd.

Take the matter of social drinking.
More and more this is motivated by the desire to satisfy the
requirements of sociability—and too many young people are
facing the ultimatum:
"Drink . . . or be left out . . .
No drink . . .
no dance . . .
no date!"

If you decline a drink, you are accused of assuming a "holier-
than-thou" attitude,
you are not a "good sport."
You are a wet blanket.
The refusal to drink is often interpreted as a boorish criticism
of the occasion and those conducting it.

Social pressure is a dreary fact of our day, and you young
people who try to buck it run into embarrassing situations and
feel certain tensions that result in strained relationships.

Now it is a natural human desire to be congenial with the group and to act in harmony with prevailing customs, and the liquor trade is exploiting it to the limit.

It is this social pressure that induces you to begin drinking.
It is not because you are thirsty
 or like the taste of alcohol
  or the smell of it,
but simply because you lack the conviction that will enable you to be "different."
You don't want people to think that you are "queer."
The drinking which is required by the powerful pressure of an authoritative social code is a type of tyranny.
This tyranny of the crowd is actually a flagrant interference with your personal liberty and a gross repudiation of the democratic principle and spirit.

Why is it that people who want to imbibe alcoholic beverages insist that you take one too, just to be sociable?
But do they likewise insist that you are
   a spoil-sport,
   a wet blanket,
   a prude,
if you decline a cup of coffee or prefer a cup of tea?

I am not suggesting that you isolate yourself from social situations to avoid the embarrassment of refusing a drink.
Not at all! This was not Jesus' viewpoint.
He Himself was criticized because He associated with all types and manner of people.

No . . . instead refuse that drink and then show the others that you can have as much fun as anyone.
In fact, the nondrinker should have more fun, for alcohol eventually dulls the brain and acts as a depressant.

I can never understand why the person who acts on principle
should be considered dull.
There is excitement in taking a stand . . . in being different.
It brings a sparkle to the eyes.
    The mind is alive.
       The spirit sings.
          True values come into sharper focus.

Yet when one falls into line . . . going along with the crowd,
conforming to the group pattern, nothing new is happening!
            There is weary repetition,
          dull compliance
        lack of initiative
      boredom.

And that is exactly what so many of you are feeling
    and why so many of you are dissatisfied with life.
Have you ever stopped to wonder *why* you have not wanted to
be different?
Is it because you have not found yourself . . .
          who you are . . .
        why you are here . . .
      where you are going?
So you think that your protection and security lies in huddling
together with your friends,
    losing your unsure self in the group.

The problem is that by losing yourself in the group, you can
go through your whole life and *never* get the answers to what
you are supposed to do with your life.

Then too, what "everyone else" is doing may be quite wrong.
Many students cheat, but that does not make cheating right.
Remember that it is the *mob* that lynches an innocent man.

Entire nations have swallowed evil propaganda which was all
falsehood.
The fact that millions believed it did not turn falsehood into
truth or avert disaster.
In fact, what governments decide can be—and often has been
—quite wrong.

Henry Thoreau—a rugged New England individualist of the
nineteenth century—once went to jail rather than pay his poll
tax to a state which supported slavery.
During this period he wrote his essay "Civil Disobedience"—
now famous the world over.

Thoreau's good friend, Ralph Waldo Emerson, hurried to visit
him in jail, and peering through the bars exclaimed:
    "Why, Henry, what are you doing in there?"

The uncowed Thoreau replied, "Nay, Ralph, the question is,
what are you doing out there?"
Who is the queer one—Little Bron or his governess?
            Thoreau in jail—or the rest of us outside?

Thoreau was not a churchman because he thought the churches
of his day too convention-bound—and perhaps he was right.
Yet in his book *Walden* he speaks often of God.
He explains that he went to Walden Pond to live the simple
life because he wanted to get just those answers that you and I
seek:

> "I went to the woods because I wished ... to front only
> the essential facts of life and see if I could not learn
> what it had to teach, and not, when I came to die,
> discover that I had not lived...."

At another time this amazing man commented:

"If a man does not keep pace with his companions perhaps it is because he hears a different drummer. Let him
step to the music which he hears, however measured or
far away."

Any man or woman who accomplishes anything worthwhile
must have the courage to be different, even to be regarded as
queer, because they are marching to the drumbeat of a Different Drummer and they are not afraid to be out of step.

Abraham Lincoln was one who listened to the Different
Drummer, and not to the vindictive voices of his advisers.

Stephens, Phillips, and Beecher were among Lincoln's contemporaries who were echoing the cry "Crush the South..."
"Stamp out the whole slave-holding aristocracy...
    Make them pay to the last acre of land,
        the last vestige of power,
            the last drop of blood."

But the great man upon whose furrowed brow the responsibility rested, heard a Different Drummer...

    "With malice toward none, with charity for all, let us
    strive on to finish the work we are in, to bind up the
    nation's wounds...
    to do all which may achieve and cherish a just and lasting
    peace among ourselves and with all nations."

What is the verdict of today?
Whose words are remembered and repeated—
Lincoln's or Stephens'?

Woodrow Wilson was another.

As a son of the manse, he knew how to listen to the voice of God, and he was not afraid to take a position that other men, hearing no distant drumbeat, delighted to ridicule.

When Wilson went to Paris after the first world war, his consuming passion was to work out a peace on a just and righteous basis.
Someone sneered that Wilson talked like Jesus Christ.
Could there have been a greater compliment paid to any man?
But it was not intended as a compliment.

In our day—as in Wilson's—there are many who are not at all certain that they want to be like Christ.
Most of their opinions of Him are formed out of puerile ignorance and a tangle of mistaken conceptions.

Yet Christ Himself would be the first to tell you that this is a central issue you need to face honestly—
        before you dare call yourself a Christian.
Jesus never deceived anyone about the cost of following Him.
Over and over He asserted that what He was offering was hard,
        that a man had better sit down and count the cost before
        deciding to become one of His disciples.
He offers a cross—not a cushion.
He recruits men—not weak-kneed boys.

And He would have stern words for the minister who pleads with people to join his church,
        as if they were doing the church a favor ...
who sets the requirements for church membership so low that people can fall over the threshold.

Yet Jesus did not ask us to be different just to make life hard.
He was thinking of our happiness when He said:

"Woe unto you, when all men shall speak well of you. . . ."
Luke 6:26

Why . . . "Woe unto you?"
Isn't it all right to be thought well of?
Isn't popularity a fine thing?

Yes, popularity is pleasant.
I like it as much as you do.
But the truth is no man can have any convictions
                    or stand for any principles,
                        or stick to any standards at all,
and be liked by everyone.

Jesus put it this way:

> "How on earth can you believe while you are forever
> looking for each other's approval and not for the glory
> that comes from the one God?"   *John* 5:44

It always amazes me the way people come to church, partici-
pate fully in the prayers and rituals, nod in agreement during
a sermon on faith and prayer.

Yet if the same people were sitting socially at home that Sunday evening talking about the problems of our time—and if
someone said impulsively, "Let's pray about this"—there
would be a most uncomfortable silence.
The one who suggested prayer would be considered a little
queer—different.
We preach about having faith and vision—yet when somebody
shares a daring dream with us,
        presents us with an exciting and thrilling vision,
we think he is a bit peculiar.

We hold up certain ideals, and when in society a young man

or a young woman takes a stand for these ideals, even to the point of making the rest of us uneasy, we think that he or she is an oddball.

We say that we believe that God can lead people, and that His guidance is available in everything...
Yet when certain people try to seek His guidance in planning a vacation
　　　in picking a college
　　　　　or in selecting friends,
we conclude that they are queer.

There is another reason why Jesus said

　　　"Woe unto you when all men speak well of you."

As our fear about others' approval grows, our freedom shrinks.
We can see this at its most extreme in the totalitarian state.
The totalitarian state cannot exist unless it is composed of de-individualized persons.
There the citizen gives up one of Christianity's most outstanding characteristics: the freedom of choice.

It is literally true that only in God's will do we have the chance to find ourselves, to be persons.
Therefore only in God's will do we have real freedom.
Today the world has a desperate need of people who are willing to be different.

In Bernard Shaw's play *St. Joan*, some soldiers are talking about the "Maid of Orleans."
One of them says, "There is something about—the girl . . . .
Her words and her ardent faith in God have put fire into me."
His captain replies, "Why, you are almost as mad as she is."

And the soldier stubbornly goes on, "Maybe that's what we
need nowadays—mad people.
See where the sane ones have landed us."

If it is sanity that has brought the world to its present state . . .
    if it is sanity that has produced the social order in which
    we live . . .
then I for one am willing to give madmen a chance.
I believe we need people who are different.

All those who have carried civilization forward have been
angry men—grousing in the public parks and the market
places, nailing denunciations up on public buildings.
They knew they were in a conflict, and they took the wrongs
in society—yes, and the wrongs in the church—
    terribly to heart.

We need such people who will carry their faith into the office
                             into Congress
                      into society
                into the school
            into the home . . .
people who will be different even if it will cost them their
social popularity
    their economic fortunes,
      or their very lives.

But one does not get that kind of faith except by a personal
friendship with Jesus Christ.
Then He will tell you what to do.
    You will be sure of your ground.
      With His hand on your shoulder, you will have no fear
      of the opinion of other people.

Easy? Of course it is not easy.
I think too much of the youth today to offer you a sugar-coated Christianity.
That would betray my Lord.
It would also not be worthy of your great potential.

If I can read the signs of the times at all, you are more than a little satiated with softness,
     with having everything handed to you,
     so that you know the value of nothing.
You have contempt when the church contents itself with glad-handing.
Deep in your hearts you look with longing toward the heights.
You know that there will be rugged terrain,
               panting lungs,
             aching legs,
but also the cool, clean upper air and the exhilaration of gaining the summit at last,
     of achieving vision and perspective.

God's marching orders always involve sacrifice and courage.
The drumbeat of the Different Drummer calls for bravery.
It is not for dancing.
It does not appeal to the blood—but to the heart of a person.
It calls for will and sacrifice.
It is a stirring drum, and they who hear it are always in a minority.

Those who answer it may perchance hear the words of a new Beatitude . . .

    "Blessed are they who are thought queer, for they have taken the gospel to heart."

·VI·

❧ It was the summer of 1949. My nine-year-old son, Peter John, and I had been shopping on Princes Street in Edinburgh —not for Braemar sweaters or fine tartans—but for toy soldiers. As we looked over the colorful, carefully wrought figures —the Argyle and Sutherland Highlanders, the Beefeaters, the Black Watch, the Seaforth—I was as fascinated as my son. Of course something was missing from the moment; Big Peter should have been there with us. Such a walking compendium of knowledge about the British regiments he had been! And he had looked forward to this trip, but the final tap on the shoulder had come for him the January before.

Peter John poured out on the counter the money he had been saving. There was enough for three boxes of the soldiers. Proudly he walked out of the store with the package under his arm, and we boarded a trolley car. It was only after we had gotten off at our stop and were walking along the street that Peter John realized that he had left his package on the car. He stood disconsolate, staring in the direction the tram had disappeared. For a little boy, it was a great loss.

"Edinburgh is a large city," I told him. "We'll try to get the soldiers back, but you shouldn't count on it." Silently we walked on.

Minutes later we heard a Scottish voice hallooing us, "Mistress . . . Laddie. . . ." When the breathless man came in *sight, we recognized the conductor of the tram car. He must have run several blocks.*

"Laddie, we found a parcel. Is it no' yours?" And when he saw Peter John's face light up like a skyrocket, "Aye—I ken. I have a laddie o' my ain——"

And at that moment in memory I was hearing another Scottish voice explain, "In the town in Scotland in which I spent the first twenty-five years of my life . . . if you lost something on the street or in a tramcar . . . the chances were very good that you would recover it——"

This is Peter Marshall's voice—in the sermon you are about to read. He would have loved the conductor of that tramcar, as he loved all honest men.

WALLS OF STRAW

IF God is not real to you,
     and you want desperately to make Him real . . .
If you have never met Christ as a Living Person,
     and there is a deep longing in your heart to know Him
     that way . . .
If you want to overcome certain problems in your life,
     but can't seem to achieve any victory . . .
If you seek God's will for your future,
     but fail to find His guidance a reality . . .
then this sermon is for you.

It may point to the difficulty,
                    one of the causes of your failure and mine.

Sin does several things to us.
    It cuts us off from God.
        It shatters our fellowship, not because God leaves us
        but because we have left Him.
            It dulls our sense of what is right and what is
            wrong.
                It produces spiritual and moral blindness.
And it does these things just as effectively whether we are
dealing with what we call big sins or little ones.

In the town in Scotland in which I spent the first twenty-five
years of my life, there was a column each week in our weekly
newspaper listing articles found in trams,
                on the street
                in public places.

These articles had been turned in to the police station.
Always there was great variety:
    a purse containing money
      a key ring
        a rosary
      cooperative tokens
    eyeglasses
all sorts of articles handed over by the finders.

If you lost something, the chances were good that you could
recover it by going to the police station.
It was generally expected that if you found something, you
would report your find. That was the philosophy in which I
was brought up.

Suppose you lost your billfold in an American city.
What chance is there that you would ever see it again?

If, in the washroom of a restaurant, you slipped off your rings
while washing your hands, and went off and left them behind,
is it likely that you would recover them?

Would you dare lay down your handbag on the counter of a
department store, if there were other shoppers standing beside
you?
Would you risk leaving your grocery bundles just inside the
store door while you went to get your car?
If you are as trusting as that, let me warn you against it,
for in our family we have lost groceries that way.

I have observed with sinking heart that old-fashioned honesty
is a disappearing virtue.
The prevailing attitude seems to be "Finders keepers" so
that if you lose something, you are simply out of luck and can
write it off.

This lack of fundamental honesty also comes out in cheating
in school, which many of you young people admit is quite
widespread.
Many of you who believe in God and are active in church still
see little or no connection between religion and honesty.

I am told that athletes accept under-the-table payments
cheat in academic work
"crib" on examinations.
And then you shrug and comment that it is "done" . . . to be
expected.
And even where an Honor System exists, many of you say that
you would not report another student—no matter what pledge
you have signed.
"None of my business" is your feeling.

Part of what is behind all the cheating in our schools is the conviction that in order to secure a good job, a college degree is necessary—by hook or crook.
It is the utilitarian view of education.

The cheater only cheats himself—out of the solid values of learning, the joy of new ideas, enlarging intellectual horizons,
   the privilege of dipping into the great minds of other times,
      the satisfaction of accumulating knowledge
      and wisdom.

Then there is lying—many forms of lying.
To be sure, as you young people look out on our world, everywhere you see older people setting you a miserable example.

It is a shocking thing to realize that witnesses, after being sworn in, will yet persist in telling lies.
There are the lies many people seem to feel justified
      in order to get a job or Social Security benefits . . .
                  lies about their age,
                  their experience,
                  how long they held the last job.
The temptation to be dishonest, however, seems particularly strong when we are making out our income tax returns.
This is fast becoming a national disease.

No, you are not guilty of these particular lies, of course.
But before you begin to glow with self-righteousness, let me ask if we—you and I—would be willing to look with God at our own lives.

It is not easy to confront ourselves.

Most of us have had long practice in avoiding this at all costs.
We make excuses.
We say, "But what I did is nothing compared to what So-
and-So does all the time."
    We rationalize.
        We blame others.

We insist that we could not help certain situations, when we
did absolutely nothing to prevent these situations from arising.
We mutter something about being unlucky—
    getting all the bad breaks.
        Things are never our own fault.

One reason why so many of us are unhappy and worried is that
we are in a state of civil war.
We are at war with ourselves.
It is an age-old conflict.

As Paul puts it:

> "I cannot understand my own actions;
> I do not act as I want to act;
> On the contrary, I do what I detest. . . .
> I cannot be good as I want to be,
> and I do wrong against my wishes. . . .
> Miserable wretch that I am!
> Who will rescue me from this body of death?"
>
> *Romans* 7:15,24

I am preaching this sermon to myself, and to as many of you
as will join me in a confession that we are not honest with
ourselves and, what is worse, we are not honest with God.
God—whether we like it or not—is a moral righteous Being.
We can have His help with our life and affairs only on His
terms.

And His terms are square-dealing,
    absolute honesty.

Our wrong-dealings, small or great, eat into our faith like
acid . . .

> "And whatsoever we ask, we receive of Him, because we
> keep His commandments and do those things that are
> pleasing in His sight."   *I John* 3:22

Ah, that's just our trouble.
So often we know perfectly well that we are not doing things
pleasing to a righteous God, and so we have no faith at all
that He will help us with schoolwork,
                or in our social life,
           or help us find His guidance for a job,
       or overcome habits which are defeating us.

Our trouble, you see, is not intellectual or theological.
It is moral.
The strange thing is that so often, when this is our problem,
we are still fascinated with Christ and His gospel.
We can't give ourselves to Him of course, but we can't quite
let Him go.
So we take comfort in long-winded intellectual discussions
about religion.

I have watched this with young people at summer conferences.
They adore lengthy bull sessions, about life in general,
                      and religion in particular.
They want to discuss the so-called conflict between science
and religion . . .
Comparative religions . . . "What right have we to claim that
Christianity is superior to other religions?"
> "What about those who have never heard of Christ?
> Are they lost?" . . .

They want to talk about war and peace and "the bomb"—
and about weighty theological matters like predestination,
when all the time the real issue is their own personal relationship to Jesus Christ.

I have watched the same thing with some of you who come
to my office for personal conferences.
Very rarely is the real trouble what you say it is.
"I can't get along with my mother and father," said one
sixteen-year-old girl.
"They're not fair to me."
What was really wrong was that beginning in the fifth grade
she had been taking money out of her mother's purse, at first
coins, and then bills in larger and larger amounts.
This had weighed on her mind until the guilt was even inter-
rupting her sleep at nights.

"I can't join the church," a college student told me, "because
intellectual honesty won't let me subscribe to all the creeds.
I want to discuss this with you."
But when we got down to discussing it, the boy's real agony
was that he had deliberately lied to a high school girl and
led her down the primrose path.
He had had an affair with her by promising her marriage, then
had abandoned her to try the same ruthless technique with
another girl.

So, you see, the issue in Christianity, in spite of what some
people say, is not usually an intellectual one . . .
It lies much deeper than that.
It is moral.

Human nature does not change much from age to age.
Jesus Christ understands human nature—all its foibles and
dodges.
He knows our difficulty.

See how He dealt with this problem in a woman of the first
century . . .

Jesus was on His way from Judea to Galilee.
He chose the shortest route over the Great North Road,
  a route which took Him through Samaria.

Having walked all morning—a long tiring trip over the Judean
hills—Jesus and His disciples were hot and weary.
A place to sit down in the shade, and a drink of cool water
would be most welcome, they thought.

In a fork of the road, they came upon just such a place.
It was a well—Jacob's Well, tradition has it—
  shaded by a spreading tree.

The disciples went on into the nearest village, Sychar, to buy
bread, leaving Christ alone, seated on the coping of the well—
alone with His thoughts.

Around Him was country more beautiful than His native
Judea.
In the valley were clumps of walnut and olive trees.
The ground was carpeted with red anemones.

In the background, seen through a distant blue haze, were
the stony sides of Mount Gerizim with its columned temple
on top.
Overhead, the sky was a burnished copper, with the mud
houses of the nearby village baking in the shimmering sun-
light.

Nobody stirred at that hour, if he could help it.
The village streets were usually deserted.
But Jesus heard footsteps; someone was approaching.
Soon He saw a woman—her waterpot carefully balanced on
her head—coming down the road.

It was unusual for anyone to come for water in the middle of
the day.
Most women drew water in the morning . . .
    or in the cool of the evening.
Could it be that this woman wanted to avoid her neighbors?

At first the woman did not notice Christ sitting on the well-
coping in the deep purple shadow.
With a start, she saw Him as she drew nearer,
                hesitated . . .
                    and then came on.
His eyes seemed to burn into her troubled heart and she was
strangely uneasy.

"I wonder," He said, "if you would give me a drink?"
That, too, was unusual.
He was a Jew, she a Samaritan.
He was a man, she a woman.
It was all most strange and unconventional.

She expressed her surprise: "You a Jew, ask a drink of me,
a Samaritan woman?"
In order to understand the woman's surprise, we have to
remember that there had been bitter and violent enmity between the Jews and the Samaritans for some seven hundred
years.

Through the years, discontented Jews,
    would-be revolutionaries,
always found sanctuary in Samaria.
The worst insult that Jesus' enemies could hurl at Him was:
"Thou art a Samaritan and hast a devil!"
And when Jesus wanted to illustrate real compassion, which
could overcome the racial and national prejudices of His time,
He told the story of the Good Samaritan.

Also, to understand the woman's surprise, you need to understand that the etiquette of Christ's day would not permit the orthodox Jew to speak to a woman in a public place, even if she were his own wife or a relative.

No wonder the woman at the well was surprised when Jesus spoke to her so openly in such a friendly fashion.
"You a Jew, ask for a drink from me, a Samaritan woman?"

And Jesus answered, "If you only knew about a free gift God longs to give you, and who it is asking you for a drink, you would have asked Me instead. Then I would give you living water."

"What a strange man!" the woman thought.
Before that look in His eyes, she suddenly felt ashamed.
Lowering her gaze, the woman tried to brush aside her embarrassment by sarcasm:

> "The well is deep. You haven't a thing to draw water with. How on earth could you give me water? Have you some magic power? Are you greater than our father Jacob who dug this well?"

Now, His own thirst forgotten, Christ probed for the woman's real problem.
Individuals were, and still are, important to Jesus Christ.
Some of His greatest sermons were preached to audiences of one.

> "I've heard about how wonderful this water from Jacob's Well is," said Christ. "I hear that it is 'light' water, noted for its purity and flavor. But I know even more wonderful water. Whoever drinks of this water will be thirsty again.
> Whoever drinks of the water which I can give will never thirst again ..."   *John 4:13–14*

Then the woman indulged in what we would call a wisecrack: "Carrying water to and from the well is no fun. I'd like to have this water of yours so that I would never have to come to the well again."

But it was no use.

Though she evaded looking into the burning eyes, she could not throw off that penetrating glance.

She blushed suddenly when Jesus said:

"Go call thy husband and bring him back with you."

Her voice was almost inaudible as she said:

"I have no husband."

Jesus said: "That's right, you have no husband.
You have had five husbands, and the man you are living with now is not your husband."

It was evident that the shaft had gone home.

To cover her confusion, she tried to change the subject again:

"Sir, I perceive you are a prophet.
But I don't want to be selfish. Let's not talk about me.
Now what about this old argument as to where we should worship?
We Samaritans, you know, hold out for this mountain . . . and you Jews insist it is Jerusalem."

Jesus quietly but firmly answered her question with a few wise words on the nature of worship . . .

"God is spirit. The place we seek to worship Him does not matter. Real worship is to worship the Father in Spirit and reality—a communion of spirit with Spirit."

Then having gently answered her question, Christ dismissed it, and inevitably—like the wheels of judgment—came back to the first point—the real point, the wrong in her personal life

which was cutting her off from a relationship with God.
Three times the woman had tried to build walls of words,
walls of straw.
Three times Christ had knocked them down.
Now no further evasion was possible.

For a long silent moment, the woman looked into Christ's
eyes.
"I don't understand how you could know about my husbands,"
she said. "I would think that only the Messiah could know
such a thing."

Then Jesus gave to this nameless woman the most thunderous,
the most revealing words
ever caught by human ears.
Probably it was His first clear revelation of His Messiahship.
He said simply,

"I that speak unto thee am He!"   *John 4:26*

At that crucial moment, the disciples arrived back at the well.
They were surprised to find their Master talking to a woman,
especially a woman with a most unsavory reputation in the
village.
But they made no comments—asked no questions.

The woman, forgetting all about her waterpot on the coping
of the well, rushed off toward the village.
Suddenly she was seeing all of life in different colors . . .
    in fact, it had had no color for years.
The sun on her face was a golden shower.
The brown earth beneath her feet was warm and laughing.
The beat of a blackbird's wings had a rhythm caught up by
the tossing trees.

She wanted to sing or to shout.
What did she care now for gossip or what people might say!

Bursting into the home of her neighbor, she spilled out her news in a wild torrent of words.
Bubbling excitedly,
    her eyes shining
       her cheeks flushed,
her whole countenance radiating a new light,
she roused the villagers from their noontime siesta.
Some of them stood in the doorways of their houses, shading their eyes and looking in the direction of the well.
Others, more curious, hurried after the woman to the well to see for themselves.

And Jesus, seeing them coming down the road in their white robes, said to His disciples,

> "Look at them. The fields around here are already whitening for the harvest. You and I are going to do some harvesting now for eternal life in this village."

I wish we had some description, some word picture, of that nameless woman whose need gave us this story.
But, even without a description, I am sure we can see her in our minds.
We know that there must have been a look of peace on her face, such as most of us do not have.
There must have been a serenity, a joy, that we only glimpse once in a while, because—just like the woman—we spend our time and our energies building walls of straw.

We go down the road of evasion.
We travel the road of rationalization,
        of excuse and alibi,
          even of lies and deceit.
We try to fool ourselves, and we think sometimes we succeed

in fooling our enemies—even our friends—but we cannot fool
Him, for He will seek us out.

He wants—not to take away our fun in life—but to end our
inner conflicts, to give us that peace of mind in which alone
we can find real joy.

You have no desire to be plastered with a coat of whitewash or
portrayed as a saint or an angel.
You have no desire to be fitted for a halo, and you have a
horror of growing wings.

Sometimes the word *good* is given unfortunate connota-
tions . . .
"Percy is such a good boy," I have heard indulgent parents
say. "He doesn't drink. He doesn't stay out late at night.
He doesn't go out with girls. He doesn't gamble."

Always I have an insane desire to say, "But Madame, just
what *does* Percy do?"

A healthy young person despises the thought of being "goody-
goody."
I dislike it too—in that sense.
But it is a noble, a splendid thing to be *good*, sincere, clean,
and decent . . .
That is an achievement worth striving for.

There are young people who look upon Christianity as a sort
of harness which confines and restricts,
        as a garment that pinches or a hair shirt . . .
something that cramps their style and imposes severe limitations on their enjoyment of life.
To them enlistment in the ranks of the church means surrender of liberty and adherence to a long list of prohibitions
and negatives.

The Christianity I know is not negative,
> but joyously positive.
What some people do not understand is that those young people who have truly met Jesus Christ have embarked on a wonderful adventure . . .
> They have found the reality of His Presence . . .
> They have accepted His advice for their lives,
>> His guidance for their choices,
>> His solving of their problems.

And they have found all these wonderful gifts because they were willing to pay a price.
They have honestly called the roll of their sins . . .
> their laziness,
> their cheating,
> their bad temper,
> their tawdry use of sex,
> their selfishness,
> their vanity and greed,
and found—not only that they are forgiven—
but that they could conquer their previous habits,
lose former desires, and become, as it were, new creatures altogether.

But there are others of you who shy away from religion and make a detour around spiritual realities because you are afraid it might "get" you . . .
> afraid you might feel urges which
would transform your lives.
Afraid you might have to give up some things you enjoy too much, afraid of the adjustments which might have to be made.

Well, you are right.

True, joining the church is nailing one's colors to the mast.
But suppose you have nailed *your* colors to the wrong mast?
Or what is infinitely worse—suppose you have no colors to nail
to any mast at all?
Then for you the world is a flat featureless plane, a dull gray.
Is that your idea of a joyous life?

There is a price to be paid for spiritual reality.
It does not float down upon you, like tickertape from the
window of a skyscraper when you march in a parade.

Too long has the price of spiritual achievement been cheap-
ened.
I would not deceive you . . .
If you want God to be real to you, you have to meet His terms.
And those terms are not for cowards who want cushioned lives.

Jesus Christ walks in no moral or spiritual twilight.
In the high noon of His love there are no neutral tints.

I need to be reminded, and you need to be reminded, that
with Christ looking over our shoulders, what we do,
            how we act in the classroom,
        what we do on dates,
        how we treat our parents and friends,
    what we say and think,
are either right—or wrong.

Before you complain again that God is not real to you, I suggest that you test your life honestly and courageously by
Christ's standards,
        and then *act* on what you find.

The result will surprise you as much as it did that nameless
woman at the well of Sychar long ago.
Try it—and come out from behind your wall of straw.

·VII·

◢§ *Late one autumn afternoon two young theological stu-*
dents, David Simpson and Peter Marshall, were driving back
to Columbia Seminary in David's old Model A Ford. They
had spent the day with friends in Marietta, Georgia. There
had been a long afternoon of tennis and a rollicking evening
playing games.

"My Ford had terrible springs, and stretches of the road
were bumpy," David was to reminisce years later. "Peter was
in a talkative mood. He got started on his idea of what real
preaching should be. Vigorously he discarded merely being
a conscientious student of other men's work; writing sermons
by putting their thoughts and quotations together like a patch-
work quilt.

" 'That's not good enough,' I remember he said, 'no
matter how fine the stitches or how careful the workmanship.'

"He talked about what he called 'pictorial preaching.'
As Peter warmed to his subject, his Scottish brogue got thicker
and thicker. . . .

" 'Look, David—isn't the problem of the poet, the play-
wright, the artist, the prophet, and the preacher really the
same—to make people see? What we have to do is to take
a passage of Scripture and so carefully and accurately recon-
struct the context of it that the scene comes to life. We see
it first ourselves. Then we take our listeners to the spot in
imagination. We make them see and hear what happened so

*vividly that the passage will live forever in their minds and
hearts. It's like a newsreel from the Scriptures ... a film from
the world's big drama.' " ³*

For Peter Marshall that concept of preaching hammered
out so early never changed; time merely perfected it. "Dawn
Came Too Late" is a classic example of one of his "newsreels
from the Scriptures."

DAWN CAME TOO LATE

HAVE you ever come right up to the point of making a
decision and then backed away—to your regret later on?
Perhaps it was the chance to land a new job,
> to go on a trip,
> to propose marriage,
> to take a strong stand.

The moment confronted you, made your heart beat faster.
You paused ... but did not act ... and then it was too late.
> Circumstances changed.
The opportunity never came again in quite the same way.

I have seen this happen when a man comes under Jesus' spell.
Suddenly he sees his life through Christ's eyes.
He knows that his life is off-center, purposeless.
> He feels trapped in wrongdoing.
> He lacks zest.
> He has clutched at happiness but it has eluded him.
Then he is offered the adventure of commitment to Christ.
Something stirs in him, like a bugle call to action.

He clears his throat, almost speaks, starts to move.
Then a counterforce steps in ... "Don't be hasty," it says.
                    "Let's not do anything foolish ..."
                "Watch out for embarrassment ..."
            "There's plenty of time to think it over."

But that particular moment slips by and is gone forever.
He was on the brink of a move that would have changed
everything.
He was nearly Christ's—so close to greatness.

                But nearly is not enough.

It has happened so from the dawn of time.
The story of Nicodemus is the story of such a man ...

He might have been a disciple—but was not.
Nicodemus was a member of the Sanhedrin—the highest
Jewish court.
The label John gave Nicodemus has stuck ...
        "Nicodemus, which at the first came to Jesus by night."
Why did Nicodemus wait until it was dark?
Was he, perchance, afraid?

Suppose Nicodemus came while it was night simply because
he could wait no longer ...
Suppose he had come—without wasting a minute—
        immediately after he had seen Christ for the first time?

Nicodemus knew the spot well.
He had sometimes sought refreshment of the spirit there himself when he could no longer stand either the heat of Jerusalem
                            or its seething intrigue.

The tall man drew his beautiful outer cloak of striped linen
more closely about his shoulders.

It was frosty at night on the Judean hills.
He paused on the brow of Olivet to look out across the moon-
lit valley.
The Temple, which Herod was still rebuilding for the Jews,
towered over the valley of Jehoshophet and Hinnom,
    gleaming like snow in the moonlight.
Nicodemus sighed involuntarily as he looked down at the city.
Asleep, Jerusalem looked peaceful enough.
    But awake? It was a dirty city . . .
            a desperate city . . .
The dignified aristocrat knew only too well the machinations
at its heart.
The Nazarene—whether He knew it or not—was in real danger
of His life.

Stepping out of the shadows, Nicodemus found Christ exactly
where Joseph had said he would.
Strangely, the Master seemed not at all surprised to see him.
In fact, it was almost as if He were expecting Nicodemus.

They talked for hours—those two—totally unaware of the
passing of time.
There was a meeting of minds such as Nicodemus had never
known even in his youth, with his greatest teachers from
Jerusalem, Corinth, or Alexandria.
In the Lord of Life, this master of Israel discovered fathomless
depths of mind and heart.

Nicodemus knew men.
"Here is no cheap fanatic," he thought.
"Here are clear eyes and a quiet voice."
    "Here is Manhood at its highest."

The talk was of spiritual regeneration—being born again, but this time, not a natural but a supernatural birth.
A change in the inner man, without which no man can get into the Kingdom of God.

At this point, Nicodemus asked what any one of us might have asked,
"How can a man be born when he is old?"   *John* 3:4

You and I have voiced the same doubts in different ways.
Suppose Jesus asks us to give up something we want to keep—
We want to have our fun first.
"Besides, there's plenty of time."
But is there?
How do we know that there is plenty of time?

Or we have answered in another way . . .
"I am what I am—nobody special.
Even though I'm still young, I have deeply ingrained habits,
                                        not all of them good.
It just doesn't seem reasonable that I should begin all over again and be somebody else . . .
Besides, who wants to be good?
I'm just not built that way."

And Jesus has answered, "Of course you're not built that way.
I'm not talking about a little repair work here and there,
                        a little increase in kindness . . .
                    a bit more generosity.
Something much more drastic is required."

"Ye must be born again"—not by education,
                            or culture,

or legislation,
but by regeneration.

But Nicodemus was the voice of man's skeptical questioning ... "How can a man be born again?"

And Jesus answered quietly. Yes, there is a mystery here, Nicodemus, that you are not quite ready to understand.

"The wind bloweth where it listeth, and thou hearest the sound thereof, but canst not tell whence it cometh and whither it goeth: so is everyone that is born of the Spirit." *John 3:8*

There are many things going on around us which we do not understand and cannot explain ...
but they are nonetheless true and valid.

There are some things in the Christian life about which it is useless to argue, for they can never be proved by logic.
I do not fully understand regeneration.
But I have seen it take place.

I have seen men and women changed from above ... completely ...
Men reclaimed from habitual drunkenness to sobriety ...
Criminals changed into respectable citizens ...
I have seen men changed from egocentrics to outgoing men, from grasping, greedy materialists into spiritually minded men, suddenly aware of the winds of the Spirit.
And then Nicodemus asked, "How can these things be?"
Perhaps he meant, "Oh yes, I see.
All right, I believe you.
I believe that it is possible for a man to start all over.
But how? Tell me how?

How does a man begin? What does one do first?"

And then Jesus answered and said unto him—probably with a
twinkle in His eyes—
"Art thou a master of Israel, and knowest not these things?"
You, a leader of the people and don't know?
You, a teacher and interpreter of the Sacred Law and you
don't know how?

"It isn't something we can do for ourselves, Nicodemus.
Only God can work this miracle.
    He has to do it for us.
All that is required of us is our willingness to have Him make
us over.
He requires only our permission.
Our Father never violates a man's freedom of choice.
He wants for His sons only those who long to be.

"You see, Nicodemus, it is the old self-centered ego in us,
               vain,
             critical of other people,
                wanting its own way . . .
                  that is what has to go.
It's painful character-surgery, painful—but necessary.
We can give God permission to slay that self-centered person
in us, and He will.
Then the Spirit of God will come to live in us,
                          giving us a new nature,
                      a new set of desires,
                        a new way of looking at things,
                  even a new will.
                          That is being born again."

Perhaps there was sadness in Christ's eyes as He made the
strange statement that somehow, in order to achieve this re-
birth, He—this Jesus—must be lifted up from the earth.

It was beyond Nicodemus, too mysterious, this talk of the
blowing wind,
      blowing from the Unknown into the Undiscoverable ...
These beautiful words, like the music of the spheres,
falling upon his ears:

> "For God so loved the world, that He gave His only-
> begotten Son, that whosoever believeth in Him should
> not perish, but have everlasting life."   John 3:16

Christ must have felt an affinity
                  a great affection for this man Nicodemus.
For it was your visit, Nicodemus, which gave us that precious
revelation; your talk drew it forth.

You came out of your night—and a shaft of light pierced it.
You came out of your night, and now the dawn is breaking.

The two men fell silent, bound together by thoughts lying
beyond the ability of words to express.
They stood ... looking down across twenty miles of hilltops,
watching the sun come up behind the blue hills of Moab, the
misty hills.
And in the distance, cocks begin to crow.

"I must be going," said Nicodemus suddenly.
He looked into Christ's eyes and gripped His hand.
With long strides, the tall man retraced his steps down the
rocky, winding path with the parting words of Jesus still ringing in his ears—words like an echo out of eternity:

"Light has entered the world, Nicodemus, but anyone whose life is evil will avoid it; but one whose life is true will come to it, fearing it not ... Men have preferred darkness to light. It is their choice. You and I know, Nicodemus, that their decision is already made ..."

So the Master knew ...
   He knew ...

Time passed.
It was now late in September—the time of the Feast of Tabernacles.
Many things had happened since that night when Nicodemus had first come to the Galilean.
Many people had been healed ...
   many miracles wrought ...
      many words spoken ...
         many prayers uttered ...
many plots hatched, many schemes perfected.

The Pharisees were increasingly troubled by the following Jesus had attracted because of His miracles.
Many of the common folk were actually beginning to believe that He was, indeed, the Messiah—even as He had said.
That would not do!

On the last day of the Feast, the seventy-one members of the Sanhedrin solemnly assembled in the great Hall of Hewn Stone in the Temple.
Caiaphas had called them into session.
The question was: "What shall we do with Jesus?"

The discussion rose and fell like waves around the semicircle of distinguished men.

Caiaphas seemed impatient of discussion.

It was apparent that he wanted Christ put to death.

But some said, "Not yet. On what basis could you condemn Him now?"

Others sided with Caiaphas.

Anger—a quiet cold anger—welled up in Nicodemus.

He was hearing once again the faint sigh of wind through cypress trees,

> feeling a hand on his shoulder...

> > seeing the pink dawn beyond a distant hillside...

hearing a quiet voice saying, "But he that doeth truth cometh to the light."   *John* 3:21

Suddenly Nicodemus felt that his own future was not important.

Did it matter what his compatriots thought of him?

Nothing mattered except honesty,

> > > fairness,

> > justice,

> > truth.

And Nicodemus rose from his stone chair and pulled himself to his full height.

A voice, calm, clear, used to controlling other men, rang out through the marble hall:

> "Surely our Law does not condemn the accused before listening to his defense, calling reputable witnesses, and ascertaining the full truth..."

Caiaphas rose in his place—mockery in his eyes,

> > a sneer on his lips:

> "Are you a Galilean too? Nothing good comes out of Galilee. I'm surprised at you, sir. Is this some kind of

September madness of yours?"

Nicodemus did not reveal to the Sanhedrin that he was willing
to stand with Christ whatever happened.
He did not announce that he was willing to follow Him and
trust Him all the rest of the way.
No—he did not do that. But he had spoken!
He had sought to defend Him on a point of Jewish law!
He had taken one step toward the light!

There was a strange peace in the heart of Nicodemus.
Already he felt those eyes, warm and appreciative, smiling
upon him.

Only once more do we see Nicodemus.
It is near the end of the narrative, some five months later.
The scheming Caiaphas has had his way: Judas had played into
his hands.

The Master had mounted His last pulpit . . .
     preached His last sermon.
The beggars waiting by the gates of Jerusalem would still need
their crutches and sticks, for He who might have freed them
from dependence on those extra legs was Himself dead.

After hatred had finished its work, "Joseph of Arimathæa,
being a disciple of Jesus, but secretly for fear of the Jews,
besought Pilate that he might take away the body of Jesus:
and Pilate gave him leave . . ."   *John 19:38*

He had prepared a rock-hewn tomb that the Master might be
interred with love and tenderness and that deep inarticulate
sorrow which had stunned the little band of believers.

Joseph came therefore, "and took the body of Jesus. And there
came also Nicodemus, which at the first came to Jesus by

night, and brought a mixture of myrrh and aloes, about an hundred pound weight. Then took they the body of Jesus, and wound it in linen clothes with the spices . . ." *John 19:38–40*

"And there came also Nicodemus . . ."
There is a sob in John's words.

Nicodemus, who first came by night, now comes in daylight.
But it is too late.
He can do nothing for the Master now except lavish the spices on His body, and wish that he might have saved Him.

The Master had said that it was hard for a rich man to get into the Kingdom.
So Nicodemus found it . . .
He had much to lose by taking a definite stand.
But he should have had the courage; now he knew it.

There in the Sanhedrin he should have said, "Yes, I am one of His disciples. I believe that what He says is true.
I had a long talk with Him. I have never met a saner Man,
a kinder Man,
a wiser Man.
Go ahead, excommunicate me too.
I intend to stand with the Galilean to the end."

Instead he had taken but one timid step toward the light, and that had not been enough to stem the dark tide.

Nicodemus might have stood with John, there at the foot of the Cross, when the others crouched at the fringe of the crowd, ready to run at the first sign of danger.

When the others forsook Him and fled, Nicodemus might have been there . . . stood by Him, for the sake of that night when they had together watched the dawn come up over the hills of Moab.

Now it was too late.
    The Master was dead . . .
        "And there came also Nicodemus . . ."
            His tears lay on the white linen like diamonds.

Many of you—like Nicodemus—have come close to Jesus.
Perhaps you too have felt the nudge . . .
    the uneasy feeling in your own conscience . . .
        the tugging at the heart . . .
            the resolves that spring up every now and then . . .
            the longing to do something special . . .
                to *be* someone . . .
Could not that be Christ calling you?

And you have waited . . .
    You wanted to respond . . .
        but you waited.

Remember that He will not force Himself upon you.
He will not assault you, or intrude where He is not wanted.
Christ will let you go through the years, using no restraint or
compulsion beyond the appeal that He is constantly making—
    to your better nature,
        to your loyalty,
            your gratitude,
                your recognition of the imperishables,
the hunger of your own young heart.

There are some terrible scenes in the Gospel narrations:
Jesus standing and letting the rich young ruler walk away from
Him.

And if the Gadarenes prefer their swine to His company,
He does not argue the point . . .
He enters the boat again . . .
    The wind fills the sails,
      slowly the vessel draws out.
        He goes as silently as He came.

If the inhospitable Samaritans do not want Him, He punishes
them in a far more terrible way than the disciples suggested:
They were for calling down fire from heaven on them.
Jesus does something more awful . . .
    He simply passes on and leaves them.

An hour may come when you will never again hear Christ's
knock on your heart's door . . .
Everything that happens to you from now on—in this life and
throughout eternity—hinges on whether or not you stretch
out your hand to open the door to Him.
The latch is on the inside.

Just one more step, Nicodemus.
Just one more step to take.
The dawn is coming.

It must not come . . . too late!

·VIII·

◆§ *There was a boy who grew up in a town called "the Iron Burgh" because it is the center of the Scottish iron trade—Coatbridge, eight miles east of Glasgow. The child's environment was that of fire, smoke and soot . . . the roar and rattle of massive machinery . . . the flames of the furnaces on the night skies. A network of railways fanned out from the town to transport the finished boilers, firebricks, railroad wagons, the malleable iron.*

As the boy grew, he wandered farther afield. He saw Clydeside where so many ocean giants are built, with the tall cranes and the davits poking into the sky. He stood on the bank of the narrow, man-made canal listening to the sound of hammers and riveters, the yelping of the tugs. And his imagination soared. From there he could go to any spot in the world . . . the South Seas . . . China . . . Africa . . . India . . . Why not?

Often he bicycled to Blantyre where the missionary-explorer David Livingstone had been born. He would wander into the tiny stone cottage where David had lived. The beds were bunks in the walls with curtains pulled across them to shut out some of the bitter cold. David had gone to work in a cotton mill at ten, but he had taken his Latin book with him —and his dreams. The dreams must have reached far beyond Blantyre, the wee cottages and the mill. For he took one of the boats from Clydeside one day. He explored the heart of the Dark Continent, found the Zambesi River and Victoria Falls. He dealt a staggering blow to the African slave trade. His tired heart was buried in an African jungle, the rest of his body in Westminster Abbey.

As the boy pondered all this, he knew that what had happened to David Livingstone and to many of his fellow countrymen—adventurers, conquerors of new frontiers, colonizers—had not been happenstance. Something (was it God?) planted the dream of destiny in a man's heart, and he went out in faith to meet that dream. Then it was important that the vision be worthy. There was a risk in reach.... Certainly there had been plenty of risk for Livingstone, but ah, the adventure ... the deep inner satisfactions of contributing something to the world! Then anything was possible with a dream big enough and God's will behind the dream.

The boy who roamed and pondered was Peter Marshall. He was to reach and to risk far beyond the horizons of his native land. Yet always he would carry in his heart an undying love for Scotland: for the Doric and the "braid Scots" tongue; for Celtic love songs and poetry; for the sturdy independence of the sons of the heath; for the mists, the windswept moors with heather slanting, the low stone cottages; for "his ain folk."

THE RISK OF REACH

IT was an afternoon in the early summer; there was a strange quiet on the battlefield.

In the bright sunshine, the air was balmy and had a breath of garden in it.

By some grotesque miracle, a bird was singing somewhere near at hand.
On the firing step, with his rifle lying in a groove in the parapet, stood a private soldier in field-gray, his uniform stained with mud and blood.

On his face, so young yet strangely marked with the lines of war that made him look old, was a wistful faraway expression.

He was enjoying the sunshine and the quiet of this strange lull in the firing.
The heavy guns had been silent—there was no sound to break the eerie stillness.

Suddenly a butterfly fluttered into view and alighted on the ground almost at the end of his rifle.
It was a strange visitor to a battleground—so out of place—so out of keeping with the grim setting
      rifles and bayonets
    barbed wire and parapets
  shell holes and twisted bodies.

But there it was—a gorgeous creature, the wings like gold leaf splashed with carmine,
swaying in the warm breath of spring.

As the war-weary youngster watched the butterfly, he was no longer a private in field-gray.
He was a boy once more, fresh and clean, swinging through a field in sunny Saxony, knee-deep in clover
                  buttercups
               and daisies.

That strange visitor to the front-line trench recalled to him
the joys of his boyhood, when he had collected butterflies.
It spoke to him of days of peace.
It was a symbol of the lovelier things of life.
It was the emblem of the eternal, a reminder that there was
still beauty and peace in the world—that somewhere there
was color and fragility
   and perfume
  and flowers
 and gardens.

He forgot the enemy a few hundred yards across no man's land.
He forgot the danger and privation and suffering.
He forgot everything as he watched that butterfly.

With all the hunger in his heart,
with the resurrection of dreams and visions that he thought
were gone, he reached out his hand toward that butterfly.

His fingers moved slowly, cautiously, lest he frighten away this
visitor to the battlefield.
In showing one kind of caution, he forgot another.
The butterfly was just beyond his reach—so he stretched,
forgetting that watchful eyes were waiting for a target.

He brought himself out slowly—with infinite care and pa-
tience—until now he had just a little distance to go.
He could almost touch the wings that were so lovely.

And then ... ping ... *ing* ... *ing* ... *ing* ...
A sniper's bullet found its mark.
The stretching fingers relaxed ...
  the hand dropped flat on the ground ...
For the private soldier in field-gray, the war was over.

An official bulletin issued that afternoon said that
    "All was quiet on the Western Front..."
And for a boy in field-gray it was a quiet that no guns would
ever break.[4]

There is always a risk—when you reach for the beautiful.
When you reach out for the lovelier
                finer
                    more fragrant things of life—
there is always a risk—and you can't escape it.

The risk is what makes the Christian life exciting.
    It is thrilling—make no mistake about it.
      It is an adventure.
As long as we live in this world, there will always be a risk in
reach.

But there are many in our time who are abnormally afraid of
that risk of reach.
They are afflicted with a modern disease.
The psychiatrists have ponderous names for the sundry phobias
that afflict us poor humans...
and the names are as terrible as the disease.

Agoraphobia is the fear of open spaces...
while claustrophobia is the fear of being shut in...
and acrophobia is the fear of heights.
There are many people who are afraid to climb...and they
will not leave the ground...
    to get out on the roof of a building
      or up in a tower
        or on a mountain.
To be up on any elevation and look down makes them dizzy,
    affects their sense of balance,

strikes terror into their hearts.
They are afraid of that which is high.
They have acrophobia.

But acrophobia is not only the fear of high monuments
                              mountains
                              and flights in airplanes.
                    It may also be the fear of high ideals
                              high thoughts
                                   high ambitions.

There are timid souls who avoid high places because they are
afraid . . .
But then there are others who avoid high ideals because they
are content with low ones.
There are persons who do not have high ambitions because
they are lazy.
Altogether there are a great many people afflicted with acrophobia.
Are you?

Not enough of you today are hitching your wagons to stars.
You think it enough to couple a trailer to your car.

Jesus remarked upon those who sought the small and shallow
things of life,

   "Verily, I say unto you, They have their reward."
                                   Matthew 6:2

That is, they got what they went after, and that is all they will
ever get.
That is what they deserve.

They take a tin thimble to the ocean and scoop up a few
drops, for that is all they can get into a thimble.
It isn't the fault of the ocean they did not get more . . .
that they did not plunge in and swim in the ocean's immensity.

The tragedy of this age is that people with minds to think and
souls that are hungry are so afraid to reach up and seek the
things that are high.
What a tragedy that personalities in this glorious twentieth
century are afflicted with acrophobia.

The night sky does something to the star-gazer.
One does not remain the same after seeing a sunset,
    or gazing into the heart of a flower,
        or watching the tiny fledglings in a nest.

There is a silent uplifting importation from the Absolute.
It does us good to look up and see Orion driving his hunting
dogs across the Zenith . . .
Or Andromeda shaking out her tresses over limitless space.

It enlarges the self to have studied great architecture . . .
    to know great art—the reds of Titian
        the sunsets of Turner
        the seas of Winslow Homer . . .
to have felt the spell of epic deeds . . .
to have swung to the rhythmic pulse of Homer . . .
to have trembled with the passion of Romeo
    or the tenderness of Francis of Assisi.

To have wrestled with Kant's categorical imperatives,
    the whirring of angels' wings in Milton's *Paradise Lost,*
to have been swept away on the surge of music in Beethoven.
To have engraved upon the heart the prologue to John's
Gospel,

to march with the majestic affirmations of the Nicean Creed.

It does something inside a man.
It stretches him mentally,
    stirs him morally,
        inspires him spiritually.
He is a bigger man—sweeter, nobler, higher,
                richer than he was before.

The uplift of adoration brings the humble but blessed beholder
to the threshold of a worship which miraculously transforms
him just by beholding.

Out of the horrors of the second world war came an expression
of such worship—a poem written by a nineteen-year-old flyer
who met his death serving with the Royal Canadian Air Force.
His father was an Episcopal rector whom I knew in Washington.
Pilot-Officer John Gillespie Magee, Jr., called his poem
"High Flight . . ." [5]

"Oh, I have slipped the surly bonds of earth,
And danced the skies on laughter-silvered wings.
Sunward I've climbed, and joined the tumbling mirth
Of sun-split clouds—and done a hundred things
You have not dreamed of—wheeled and soared and swung
High on the sunlit silence. Hov'ring there,
I've chased the shouting wind along, and flung
My eager craft through footless halls of air.

"Up, up the long, delirious, burning blue,
I've topped the windswept heights with easy grace
Where never lark, or even eagle flew—

And, while with silent, lifting mind I've trod
The high untrespassed sanctity of space,
Put out my hand and touched the face of God."

The Christian is to seek the things above—to seek them
    as the needle seeks the pole...
    as the sunflower seeks the sun...
    as the river seeks the sea...
    as the eagle seeks the ceiling of the world.

That was why Paul pleaded with the first-century Christians
to set their affections on things above...
        high things,
        lofty concepts
and "not on the things of the earth."

But it is so difficult for us to transfer our affections, for we
have fallen in love with toyland
        and our playthings have become so dear.

It is so difficult for us to believe the truth: that this life is but
a preparation for a greater and more glorious one to come...
and that if we would only believe,
    if we only had enough faith and the right kind and were
    seeking the "things above..."
all our real needs—earth's trinkets for which we strive so
desperately—would be provided for us.

Once and for all, we must put out of our minds that the purpose of life here is to enjoy ourselves
        to have a good time
      to be happy
    to make money
and to live in ease and comfort.

That is not what life is all about.
You were put here for a purpose, and that purpose is not related
to superficial pleasures.
No one owes you a living—not your parents, not your gov-
ernment, not life itself.
You do not have a right to happiness.

You have a right to nothing.
I believe that God wants us to be happy—but it is not a
                    matter of *our right*, but of His *love and mercy*.

The time for drifting
         or sleeping
         or wishful thinking
or day-dreaming is over.
The state of our world today makes that a very dangerous
pastime.

This generation of young people and all of you who are sensitive to what is going on around you, are called to a supreme
adventure.
There is a great stirring in society.
The upheavals of life and the revolutions of multitudes across
the world in desperate motion are indications that our world
can never be the same again.

So do not ever underestimate what you can do. You have the
courage to cast off your acrophobia
         and to dream big
         and to aim high—
if you do it with God's help.

Two years before I left Scotland, I had a small part in a re-
markable demonstration of what youthful vision combined
with Christian faith can accomplish.

Bert Patterson was a medical student in Glasgow University,
very much in love with Nessie Knight.
They had been friends through high school.
They were wholesome young people, interested in life
and eager to invest their personalities to some noble end.
Both belonged to a group of about twenty of us who went
around together.
We played football and cricket.
The girls had a hockey team.
We went to picnics together ... took hikes ...
Normal young people—fond of life
full of fun
with some of the virtues and most of the faults of young people
anywhere.

At last Bert graduated ...
secured his medical degree and volunteered to go to
Africa as a medical missionary.
Before he left, he and Nessie were married.
Leaving his wife at home, he then went out to establish the
Scotch Presbyterian Medical Mission at Sulenkama, Africa.

Bert knew there was nothing in Africa for him but a grass hut
and a tremendous need.
He determined to build a hospital
a dispensary
and a compound
before he could ask Nessie to come out to help him in his
work.

To those of us who were left behind there came the challenge
to do what we could to build that hospital and dispensary for
them in Africa.

Bert had gone out like a happy warrior to tramp the high road
of service and sacrifice . . .
Surely there was something we at home could do.

Money was scarce . . .
   Mission committees were hard up . . .
      The churches were giving all they could, but there were
      so many needs.

Now Nessie was quite small, but her heart was big, and she
had the spirit of a giant.
She organized us into a dramatic club to raise the money
needed to build the hospital.
She was director and coach,
      organizer and leader
of one of the craziest, maddest, and most thrilling ventures
with which I have ever been connected.

We decided to present two plays by Sir James Barrie—*Quality
Street* and *Dear Brutus.*
We determined to present the plays in one of Glasgow's
downtown theaters—the Coliseum—and to hire it for a week.

It was a fantastic sort of thing, I must admit, to think that a
gang of twenty young people could hire a theater for a week,
and do a good job of presenting such challenging plays . . .
      to do it in such a way as to raise enough money to build
      a hospital in Africa.
Nevertheless, I can only tell you what happened.

Sir James Barrie presented to us an autographed copy of the
plays that they might be auctioned and the money applied to
the fund.

Sir Horace Fellowes, a noted conductor, not only agreed to let his orchestra play, but he himself came on the opening night to conduct.

Each one of us frantically sold tickets for weeks before the production.
We enlisted all our friends in schools and in offices,
                        in restaurants and in picture houses,
                    in university and church,
                in the stores and in the tramcars.
We secured the help of the newspapers.
There was something about the whole mad enterprise that captivated our fathers and mothers.

Suffice it to say that the plays were successful beyond our dreams.
The young people acted as if they were inspired, and who can say they weren't?
And every night for a week hordes of people came to the Coliseum theater and caught the spirit of it all, so that in the end enough money was sent out to Bert to build his dispensary and a compound—a place for him to work and live.
And Nessie went out to Africa at the close of the year to join him in God's work.

Nor does the story end there.
The next year Nessie's sister, Jean, directed another of Barrie's plays, *Mary Rose*, and played the lead herself to raise enough money this time to build a hospital.

One of the Glasgow newspapers in telling the story called Bert and Nessie "Pilgrims of the Lonely Way . . ."
But I wonder if their way is so lonely after all!

Pilgrims of the Lonely Way ... Pilgrims unafraid to reach ...
They are in good company.
There are great people who walk beside them—a rich fellowship dedicated to hard labor and austere lives in far-off places.
But the excitement
       the joy
          the adventure
             the deep inner satisfactions
of those who dare to reach sky-high more than make up for
any loneliness.

For no way can be lonely if it is the way Christ walks ...
No way can be lonely if it is the way to which He calls you.

·IX·

◄§ *"The devil is real all right,"* Peter Marshall always insisted. *"I know him well. He uses insidious, diabolically clever techniques. He is dedicated to corrupting lives and keeping men and women from achieving their God-appointed goals.*

"Why is Satan always depicted as being of the masculine gender?" he liked to say. *"The devil is no fool; he changes his sex. We associate with womanhood all that is pure, lovely, sweet, and wholesome. But Satan is not above taking on the guise of what we respect in order to accomplish our downfall. Consider Delilah and Samson . . . Jezebel and Ahab . . . yes, and many a modern woman."*

He was speaking from experience. For six years after Peter's ordination to the ministry, he was a bachelor. As such, he was the target of many an aspiring maid and even some married women.

Often he received calls like this one: "Dr. Marshall, I have an urgent problem for which I need spiritual help. Could you possibly drop by this afternoon? I would come to you at the church office, only I turned my ankle yesterday." Quickly he learned to take his secretary, who would sit in an adjoining room during the conference.

Once in a series of lectures at Gettysburg Theological Seminary, Peter warned the men about the temptations that assail a minister from these designing women: "You are caught in a dilemma. If you are abrupt with them, they can accuse

152]

you of not wanting to help them. If you are courteous, they will be encouraged and make life miserable for you in many feminine ways."

When Peter was still a bachelor, one such woman had set a series of subtle traps in his way for two solid years. He had avoided them all. Finally the woman abruptly changed her tactics and confronted him in the privacy of his office with her plan to divorce her husband. She asked Dr. Marshall to join her in Mexico.

In telling me about it later, Peter said, "She couldn't understand when I spoke about my love for Christ and my responsibility to other people, so I finally told her bluntly that at that moment I found her the most unattractive woman I'd ever met. That did it!"

Of course, there were other areas where Peter wrestled with beasts in his own Ephesus.... There was the matter of using time correctly. He had no regular hours or office routine to give order to his day. He liked to stay up late; that usually meant a late start the next morning. He struggled mightily with procrastination on sermon preparation and on the serious reading that he knew he must do. Offers from other churches were attractive; did he sometimes dally with them too long?

Perhaps for him the most subtle and devastating trap of all was discouragement. When all other temptations failed, this one could always engage him in deadly battle. "Why isn't my leadership accepted?" he would moan. "Maybe I should quit, throw in the sponge."

Then was the time for us to remind one another that all discouragement is of the devil—to be recognized, fiercely re-sisted and overcome.

OUR FRIEND, THE ENEMY

To most moderns, the devil is either a swear-word
or an allusion to archaic folklore.
Nowadays the devil has become a clown in pantomime...
and hell a sardonic jest.

Quite in the mood of this gay, spoofing approach to the subject is the now-famous book *The Screwtape Letters*, written by the Oxford don C. S. Lewis.
The book is a series of letters from a senior devil, Screwtape, to his underling and apprentice, Wormwood.

Wormwood has been given the assignment of seeing to it that one average, middle-class Englishman never makes it to the Father's house.

But underneath the blithe, sparkling façade of the book, there are deep philosophical and spiritual insights.
Mr. Lewis wrote *The Screwtape Letters* not just as a humorous exercise, but for a reason.

He had important things to say:
That there is a Dark Power in our world...
That this Evil Power has intelligence and wit...
was created by God...
was once good...
and went wrong.
That on this earth there is a war to the finish between God and this Evil Power...

That we human beings are never so much in danger,

or please the Evil Power so much,
as when we do not believe that he exists, or refuse to take him
seriously.

"I know someone will ask me," Mr. Lewis writes in another
place, " 'Do you really mean, at this time of day, to re-
introduce our old friend the devil—hoofs and horns and all?'

"Well what the time of day has to do with it I don't know.
And I'm not particular about the hoofs and horns.
But in other respects my answer is, 'Yes, I do. . . .' " [6]

In so doing, Mr. Lewis places himself squarely back into the
stream of Jesus' teaching about the evil in our world.
In at least forty-three separate references recorded in the
Gospels, Jesus spoke of this Evil Personality, giving him a
variety of names:
  Satan . . .
    the Devil . . .
      the Enemy . . .
        the Adversary,
          Tempter.

A loving Heavenly Father is never the author of evil, Christ
insisted.
He attributed to this Dark Power all disease

pain
depravity
sin
and death.

Hence the devil is one to be taken seriously indeed.

One does not take lightly the one responsible for a face eaten
by leprosy with a gaping hole where the nose has been ...
    Or screaming children laid on the fiery arms of idols ...
        Or the lust for world domination that reduced hun-
        dreds of thousands of men to the level of animals
        through slavery ...
        Or the big business of prostitution.

If what Jesus had to say about the devil is true, then he is
something more than an idea for a Halloween costume.
But if what Jesus taught about the Evil One is merely superstitious nonsense, then how could we take authoritatively
anything else Christ said?

In Christ's eyes the stakes here are desperately high:
                  your immortal soul and mine,
where we shall spend eternity—either in the Father's house
or lost from ourselves, our Maker, and our fellows.

Jesus warns us that the devil's techniques are insidious.
In our time we have heard a great deal about infiltration.
But the Communists did not invent it.
It started back in the Garden of Eden when a snake slithered
his way into Paradise ...
    and this technique has been used ever since.

There is no more perfect illustration of the way infiltration
works than the Old Testament story of "Little Sunshine" or
Samson.

Any young person would have admired Samson.
He was a powerful physical specimen ...
    Head and shoulders above his companions ...
        He had the easy grace of a born athlete ...

and the wit of a toastmaster.

He loved life
	and practical jokes
		and laughter.
He was a born leader.

He had an open face, laughing and honest, a charm of personality which purchased for him indulgence rather than discipline from his parents—the discipline that might have saved him.

His mother and his father had been told before his birth that theirs was to be an extraordinary child, blessed with great gifts of body, mind, and spirit.
And so, in full anticipation of the radiant energy which would brighten their home, they named their son "Little Sunshine" or "sun-man," for that is the meaning of *Samson.*

And then, as the child Samson grew, another even more wonderful gift was added to the talents with which he had been born:
	the spirit of the Lord came upon him.

"And the Spirit of the Lord began to move him at times
in the camp of Dan between Zorah and Eshtaol."
Judges 13:25

Even from the point of view of Samson's companions, rare and awesome powers began to stir in him . . .
	not only unparalleled physical strength,
		but also the ability to sway men,
			to lead them.
And along with all this, there was his joy at being alive and

young, with the world at his feet.

He became the romantic outlaw
    the benefactor of the downtrodden
        the people's hero fighting the common enemy—the
        Philistines.
God was in the glory of this young man exulting unashamedly
in splendid strength and developing muscle.

> "Then went Samson down, and his father and his mother,
> to Timnath, and came to the vineyards of Timnath: and,
> behold, a young lion roared against him.
>
> "And the Spirit of the Lord came mightily upon him, and
> he rent him as he would have rent a kid, and he had
> nothing in his hand . . ." *Judges 14:5–6*

Can you imagine what strength it would take for a man to
subdue a lion with his bare hands.

And then we have a touch that makes Samson seem lovably
modest:

> ". . . but he told not his father or his mother what he had
> done." *Judges 14:6*

His father had always disliked braggarts.
Besides, most mothers are not fond of their darlings fooling
around with lions.
Better to keep that quiet!

Then Samson deliberately chose an insulting weapon with
which to swat Philistines:
    the jawbone of an ass.
Quite indifferent to the odds against him,

he dove into a free-for-all fracas, with the final tally at one
thousand Philistines.

So he goes cavorting through the pages of the book of Judges ...
                            full of riddles ...
                          playing tricks ...
                        and practical jokes,
with the firebrand stunt the craziest of all.

"Little Sunshine" caught three hundred foxes,
      tied them together in pairs by the tails, with a lighted
      firebrand knotted in the tails.
Then he turned the crazed animals loose into the enemy's
ripening cornfields ... vineyards ... olive orchards.

The tale must have traveled from mouth to mouth as rapidly
as the fire had spread.

Samson was now a giant in the community,
      the hero who won every contest,
         adored by the children,
            admired by the aged,
               envied by the other young men,
worshiped by the girls.

He could do no wrong—or could he?
We are not told when his downfall began, but it is not difficult
to piece the story together.
Was there ever a male hero who was not tempted by the
seductive young thing?

One common desire of youth then, as now, was to be popular,
to be sought after,
admired,
complimented,
invited here and there.
No one knows this better than the devil, for it was he who
planted these seeds in the hearts of youth.

For any of us—as for Samson—the temptation is to put ourselves first, at the center of life,
to play at being god.
"I want what I want . . ."
My will—or God's will.

In this case, God had a great plan for Samson:

> ". . . he shall begin to deliver Israel out of the hand of the
> Philistines."   *Judges* 13:5

"Little Sunshine" was meant to swat Philistines all right, but
for a better purpose than personal glory.

More than that, he was meant to be a Nazarite . . .
His body was to be kept clean of strong drink and sensual
indulgence . . .
No razor was ever to touch his head.

But the human will is always free.
God will force no man to obey Him nor will he shield any
man from temptation.
The sin is not in being tempted but in yielding.
This is our battleground, where every human being faces a
decision between God and the devil.

So Samson was tempted.
He saw a woman in Timnath, a daughter of the Philistines,
and he took it into his head that he wanted her for his wife.
His parents protested and pleaded, but the pattern had been
set years before . . .
They had never been able to resist their child's willfulness;
                                        they could not now.

The devil came to Samson in a woman's guise; he often has . . .
                                        he often does.
Samson married the girl, and it was a pathetic travesty of a
marriage, because God was not in it.
Read the story for yourself in Judges.

So Samson lost his first battle with temptation—and we can
be sure that it *was* a battle.
For God, having blessed Samson with unusual gifts, needed
him.
There had to be a tremendous battle within, particularly that
first time.

But after the first giving-in to temptation, our defenses are
weaker the next time.
We have handed over our wills to this Evil Power,
        fraternized with him like the friend he pretends to be.
He has won control.
His sly suggestions infiltrate . . .
                    then contaminate . . .
                then dominate.

    "Then went Samson to Gaza, and saw there an harlot,
    and went in unto her."   *Judges 16:1*

And so the man who with his bare hands had torn a lion limb from limb was victim of a snakebite in the tall grass of sensual indulgence.

The argument that desire alone is sufficient excuse for conduct is a philosophy as old as sex.
The unbridling of passion . . .
the exaltation of sexual pleasures torn from the context of life
and worshiped as the god of happiness—
this rationale has been given a fresh Freudian face in our century, otherwise there is nothing "modern" about it.

The temptation is always to purchase popularity by joining the crowd around the bargain counters of hell—when in exchange for an irrecoverable,
fragile,
precious thing—purity
the devil will offer the cheap, glittering baubles with which his hooks are baited.

But the truth is that the devil has no bargains.
"Take what you want, Samson.
We can settle up later . . ."

One of the devil's tricks is this:
When we choose evil, usually we get what we want at once and pay for it afterward.
When we choose good we have to pay for it first before we get it.

Most of us have found this out with as simple a matter as examinations in school.

If you chose good grades and a degree with honor, you had to
pay months ago with hard study,
    the giving up of some pleasure and recreation.

But if you chose to have a good time, you began that long ago,
and you have had your fun.
You did not pay then, but you are paying now in your frantic,
last-minute boning for your exams, and your paying is not over
yet.
There will be further deferred payments later in your life.

Make no mistake about it.
This Evil Personality is very real and very subtle.
He is real to me; I know him well.

He wants to persuade us to choose the things that we do not
have to pay for right away.
Usually they are cheap and sordid things.
"You want it," the devil says. "Charge it.
I understand. I'm your friend. Take what you want."

But the bills always come due.
And what is more, they are not all presented to you.
Payments must also be made by those close to you, bound to
you through all eternity by ties of blood and bonds of love.
In Zorah, Samson's parents would worry . . . and hope . . .
                    and pray . . . and finally grieve.

There were other women after the harlot, and finally Delilah.
Samson was still trifling with the devil's baubles.
He thought he could handle them, only to find, when it was
too late, that he had flirted with temptation too often

The story moves on.
    The scene changes.
       The music moves into a minor key.

Samson, his massive head in Delilah's lap, says, "I will go out as at other times before, and shake myself . . ."
And then as you read, you catch your breath,
for the next words are so simple,
          so terrible . . .

    "But he wist not that the Lord was departed from him."
               Judges 16:20

The Spirit of the Lord had been pushed out of a man's heart.
No man can serve God *and* the devil.
Samson had long since made his choice, had clasped the serpent to his heart.
He had had his fun; now was the day of reckoning.

The Philistines had him at last, and there was no shaking them off this time.
The repeated yieldings to temptation had sapped Samson's vital strength.

"I will go out as at other times . . ."
How often we have heard it: "I will pull myself together."
Ah, but this was not as other times:

    ". . . the Philistines took him, and put out his eyes, and brought him down to Gaza, and bound him with fetters of brass; and he did grind in the prison house."
               Judges 16:21

Bound and blind in the prison of the Philistines was Samson—

the hero meant to deliver his nation from their hands.
The true nature of the Dark Power was out in the open now.
A wrecked manhood
　　an empty shell of a person
　　　　God's great plans all awry
　　　　　　a broken heart
　　　　　　　　gaping sockets where shining eyes had been.

But in his darkness "Little Sunshine" remembered the man he
might have been . . .
　　He thought of the God he had abandoned . . .
　　　　And once more he prayed to that God:

"O Lord God, remember me, I pray thee, and strengthen
me, I pray thee, only this once, O God, that I may be at
once avenged of the Philistines for my two eyes."
Judges 16:28

It was the last cry of a desperate man.
"Remember me . . . only this once . . ."

Some part of his old strength returned to him.
Three thousand of the enemy were gathered in a great pillared
hall.
They had sent for Samson to make sport of him.
So, groping his way, he found the two key pillars of the house,
　　　　　　　　bowed himself with all his might,
and in a thunder of crashing beams, collapsing masonry, and
screaming men and women, the house fell.

The tragedy had come full circle.
The story ends with a sob . . .

　　"So the dead which he slew at his death were more than
　　they which he slew in his life."　　*Judges 16:30*

Now we begin to see why Jesus, who loves us
                        and wills the good things of life for us,
wants us to know the true nature of the Evil Power with whom
we temporize.

Then is one like Samson lost forever to his Father's house,
                              his Father's love?

We cannot know.
The one thing we do know is that—according to Jesus—
we can count on no blessed oblivion in death.
For Samson, as for all of us, the curtain comes down,
                          only to rise again.

Jesus warned us over and over that a lifetime of setting self-will
up as king . . .
        of making the wrong choices . . .
                  inevitably leads down the broad road to hell.

He spoke of "the outer darkness" . . .
              "the lake of fire" . . .
                 "the everlasting fire" . . .
Not, as we might expect, so much to the murderers, the prosti-
tutes, or the outcasts . . . but to the Scribes and Pharisees,
                 to His own disciples,
                to the church people,
               to the scholars and intelligentsia . . .
to them He had a great deal to say about hell.

You may not like it.
You may not believe in hell, but there it was, in repeated
references—on the lips of this "gentle Jesus, meek and mild."

The twentieth-century sophisticate is inclined to say conde-
scendingly, "Isn't all this merely a relic of a dark superstitious

past when bogeymen were conjured up to frighten children into being good?
"If there is a God, He couldn't possibly permit such a place.
I cannot imagine it . . .
 I cannot entertain the thought . . .
  Therefore I won't."

I remember in a humble restaurant in a poorer quarter of Atlanta, Georgia, seeing a card underneath the glass on the counter. The card said:

> "Because you don't believe in hell is no sign you ain't going there."

Despite its crudity and bad grammar, there is an underlying truth in that homely observation.
Far too often we moderns are tempted to think that just because we reject an idea, it therefore ceases to be.

Certainly we need not discuss a literal hell.
I am not concerned that you believe in a burning pit,
      a boiling cauldron,
       the devil with a forked tail,
       the smoke and the flames.
Personally, I think hell will be more terrible than that!

Suppose a soul passes through the curtain of death without the purging work of Christ—still soiled—with a record of crime
           iniquity
         sin and degradation.

Suppose that through all eternity he has to witness the playing and the replaying of his record upon earth . . .
Or to use another figure of speech, as though he were in a

motion picture house, seeing the same pictures over and over again.
Would not that be hell?

We are told in the Bible that the inhabitants of Hell . . .
those members of the lost legion . . . will be murderers,

idolators

whoremongers

sorcerers

liars.

    Now the lust to kill or to inflict pain,

to abuse sex . . .

to crave drink

or narcotics . . .

these things are of the spirit, make no mistake.
They are spiritual urges.
We sin in the flesh . . . yes, but of the spirit!

These are sins of desire . . . and we desire, not with our body, but with our spirits.
We desire with our souls, do we not?
The body supplies the vehicle of consummation . . .

the means of gratification of a base urge.

When the clock chimes for us, we leave the body behind, and it returns to the dust whence it came.

But the soul . . . what of it?
It goes on, we are told—the unsaved soul to join the lost legion . . . to swell the ranks of the hopeless outcasts.
It goes on—with its longings

its cravings

its lusts and passions—

on behind the curtain.

Suppose then, these damned souls still have their desires and lusts . . . their passions and their cravings . . . gnawing—eating —burning constantly at their personalities,
and they have no bodies with which to gratify them?
Would not that be hell?
What could be more terrible than the thought of those lost souls completely turned over to the base passions which they had deliberately chosen in life?

I think that in this connection the Old Testament injunction:
    "Choose ye this day whom ye will serve."   *Joshua 24:15*
or in the New Testament:
    "No man can serve two masters . . . God and mammon,"
has a deep significance.   *Matthew 6:24*

Let me remind you that God does not send anyone to Hell. He permits the soul a choice . . . and if a human being has chosen to gratify the lusts of the flesh rather than the longings of the spirit . . .
                that soul may have to be left with that choice!

What have you chosen?
What are you choosing—day by day?

The proof of how real Jesus knew Hell to be is that He came to earth to save us from it . . .

    "For this purpose the Son of God was manifested, that He might destroy the works of the devil."   *I John 3:8*

In other words, the reason that the God-Man came among us to live a while on the planet earth was to fight to the finish the Evil Power.

Christ gave His life to make sure of victory.

He was willing to be scourged . . .
            lashed with leather thongs studded with steel . . .
willing to be spat upon,
                smitten,
                    humiliated . . .
He was willing to be nailed to the cross with huge nails
driven through His hands and feet.

He was willing to endure such pain as we cannot imagine . . .
                    willing to burn up with thirst . . .
Willing to die suspended between earth and heaven . . .
Willing to be separated temporarily from His Father . . .
Willing to go even into hell itself.

"He was dead and buried and descended into hell . . ."
Millions in churches throughout the world repeat this every
Sunday in the Apostles' Creed.

How? Why? In what way did Jesus go into hell?
It is Peter who gives us some clues in his First Epistle.
Jesus' work of redemption on the cross would not be complete
if it included only those who were living,
            or even those who would live in future centuries.

What of those—like Samson—who had lived before?
They must hear the good news too.
They must have their chance to embrace belief.
So, says Peter, during those three days, Christ's living Spirit
went and preached "to them that are dead. . . ."   *I Peter 4:6*

They too, must know that Jesus has offered us a way out . . .
the opening of our wills and hearts and minds to His cleansing,

the giving of our lives to His safekeeping,
   the acceptance for ourselves of what He did for us on
   the cross.

Even in this, our wills are free to accept or reject.
But let us soberly consider the price we shall pay if we reject
Christ's love.

He is the only One who can deal with our sins,
the only One who can open our inner eyes to perceive the
tricks of the devil within us,
   the only One who can supply us with the strength to
   resist temptation,
      the only Friend who will never deceive us.

Others promise us sins excused
                    discounted
                    denied
            explained away.
But only at the foot of the cross do we ever experience the
beautiful divine contradiction of *sins forgiven*.

Here is the greatest miracle of all!
   that God loves men even in their hate...
      that His heart yearns for us even in our indifference...
         that His pardon and His grace are waiting for us
         even though we may feel no need of either...
            that God, for Christ's sake, is willing to forgive
            sinners such as you and me.

· X ·

&s; *I held the man's stickpin in my hand. It was not long after Dr. Marshall's death and I was going through his possessions. The tiny chip of a diamond in the pin winked at me. The story of how the pin came to be given to Peter Marshall had been told to me by our friend Marguerite. . . .*

Peter had been invited to Marguerite and Bud's for dinner. There was nothing unusual about that. Those were his bachelor days, and he dined with this particular couple so often that he even kept a pair of house slippers in their coat closet. He and Bud were making sets of Chinese Checkers to give to several mutual friends for Christmas.

On that particular night, Atlanta was in the grip of a severe ice storm with many streets impassable. Peter made it anyway.

He had no sooner gotten inside the door than he took off his shoes, put his slippers on, and asked to use the telephone. His first words over the phone were, "Are you still out of pain?"

Apparently the answer was in the affirmative because he fairly shouted for joy. It seems that the woman to whom he was speaking had been suffering acutely for months. A battery of specialists were baffled, seemingly could do nothing for her. That noon Peter had gone to her home and had prayed for her healing.

Only a few Sundays before he had been preaching on

172]

prayer—about mountain-removing. He felt that he would be a hypocritical theorist not to rise to a challenge like this woman's need. The extremity of her pain had given him bold-ness in prayer. He had suggested that together they claim Jesus' promise, "If ye abide in Me, and My words abide in you, ye shall ask what ye will and it shall be done unto you." What they had asked was that she be healed.

"I've never seen anyone more radiant or more exuberant than Peter was that evening," Marguerite told me. "So far as I know the woman was completely cured."

There was still a card in the bottom of the little box with the stickpin. The fine feminine handwriting was a bit faded. . . .

"I want you to have this gift as a tangible token of my gratitude for the mountain of illness that a loving God has removed from me."

THE ART OF MOVING MOUNTAINS

I AM sure that each of you has read this statement many times:

Prayer Changes Things.

You have seen it painted on posters which adorn the walls of our Sunday-school rooms.
You have seen it stamped on little metal plates,

read it in the Bible
heard it from the pulpit, oh, so many times.

But do you believe it?
Do you actually, honestly, believe that prayer changes things?
Have you ever had prayer change anything for you?

> Your attitudes
> your circumstances
> your obstacles
> your fears?

This is the way the Master said it:

> "... for verily I say unto you, If ye have faith as a grain
> of mustard seed, you shall say unto this mountain,
> Remove hence to yonder place; and nothing shall be
> impossible unto you."   *Matthew* 17:20

Now that is certainly one of the most audacious claims about
faith ever spoken.
Does it strike you as overstated?

Have you ever wondered why Christ chose this particular
image—moving mountains—

> to illustrate the power of faith and prayer?

He might have said something about mountain-climbing, but
no, it is mountain-*moving* which is mentioned as the expression of a robust
> virile
> and exuberant faith.

How it must grieve Him to see us go through life with such
timid attitudes toward prayer.
Constantly He was appalled at men's lack of faith ...

> "O men, how little ye trust Him!" He cried at one point.
>   *Matthew* 12:28

And in another . . .
"Why are you afraid? How little you trust God!"
Matthew 8:26

And then He promised boldly:
"If ye abide in Me, and My words abide in you, ye shall ask what ye will, and it shall be done unto you."
John 15:7

For nearly two thousand years, Christ's words have challenged men to think big . . .
to be bold for Him,
to do great and audacious works in His name.

Yet too often we do not believe His promises.
And sometimes when our prayers are answered, we do not believe even then.
We charge it off to coincidence.
We search for what we call a "logical" explanation, for we do not want to be thought peculiar.
How he grieves over our lack of faith!

But prayer is the key to Christian growth.
Through prayer, God still works His miracles today just as He did when the first Christians had the audacity to think that they could convert the world.

Do you remember when the Roman ruler of Judea—Herod Agrippa—decided to stamp out the fanatical band of men who were followers of the crucified Galilean by throwing their leader, Peter, into prison?

Herod mounted a strong guard of soldiers to keep Peter in prison until after the Feast of the Passover.
Sixteen soldiers had charge of the prisoner.

Two of them were chained to him, one on either side, and they occupied the cell with Him.

The others guarded the inner and outer doors of the prison, and Peter was secured.
He could not escape.

Meanwhile, in a house in the city, in the home of Mary, the mother of John Mark, Peter's brethren were gathered.
They were engaged in prayer.
They had been praying all week.

They were praying in earnest, praying with passionate conviction for something specific.
They were praying that Peter might be released from prison—that the Lord would somehow intervene on Peter's behalf.
Peter was sorely missed.
He was the leader.

Nearby in the prison—strange things were happening.
Gates, chains, and guards could keep out friends and keep in prisoners, but they could not prevent the coming and going of the Lord's angels.

An angel of the Lord appeared at Peter's side as he lay asleep, and a light that was not of men filled the prison.
Peter was commanded to rise up—the shackles fell from him, and he stood free of the chains that had bound him, while his two guards continued to sleep.
How was it done?
We are not told.
But the angels of God are not deterred by men.
Led by the angel, Peter followed as one in a dream, until the cool night air outside the prison brought him to the realization that he was a free man.

The church had been praying for a week that Peter might be liberated and restored to them.
Here he was, liberated; the prayer was answered.

Still musing over the strange and wonderful thing that had happened, Peter walked through the streets, deserted and still, until he came to the house which served as a meeting place of the brethren.
He knew he would find them there—praying!

Peter knocked for some time until a damsel came to the door, and hearing the voice of Peter, she became so overjoyed that she let him stand outside while she ran to the others with the good news that their leader was delivered unto them.

Upon being told that their prayer was answered, they refused to believe it and told the girl that she was mad.
But her story could not be changed.
She insisted that Peter was outside.

They next thought that it must be his ghost, because Peter was in prison—they knew—and although they had prayed earnestly that the Lord should set him free—they had not expected anything like this.
Maybe Herod had already killed him!
They thought of every possibility—save that they had gotten what they had been praying for.

The question naturally arises: Why were they praying at all? Their skepticism clearly demonstrated that they did not expect an answer.

We are not much better today after nineteen centuries of practice in the art of prayer . . .

Not much more expectant after two millenniums of answered petitions.
We have not much more faith . . . perhaps not as much.

We are like the old lady whose view from her front porch was spoiled by an unsightly hill that not only had no beauty itself but also shut out much of the beauty that lay beyond.

The old lady wished again and again that the hill might be removed, and then she came upon the promise in Scripture, Mark 11:23.

> "For verily I say unto you, That whosoever shall say unto this mountain, Be thou removed, and be thou cast into the sea; and shall not doubt in his heart, but shall believe that those things which he saith shall come to pass; he shall have whatsoever he saith."

She decided to try, and one night she prayed that the hill might be removed.
Next morning when she arose, her first thought was to go to the window and look out to see whether or not the Lord in the night had moved the hill.

Her comment was most revealing, and revealed why her prayer —like most of ours—was unanswered. Said she, "Umph, well, it is still there, just as I expected."

We really do not believe in prayer.
Even as we pray, we do not expect results . . . and we hardly know why we bother to pray at all.

I have seen what prayer can do on many levels.
Take the matter of jobs—economic needs . . . down-to-earth things.

When I first landed in this country, at the Battery off Ellis
Island, I had just enough money to last me two weeks.
So I immediately went after a job in New York City.
I was told that there were some openings in a steel construc-
tion job.
Still another skyscraper was going up . . .
When I applied, I was told that I could have a job on two con-
ditions.
The first was that I had to join a union.
That was all right; I did not mind that.
But then the hiring man added, "See that guy over there? The
one with the plaid flannel shirt? You have to pay him fifty
dollars."

At that point, I did some quick thinking and praying.
And I decided that bribing someone to give me a job,
                                      indeed buying a job,
                                         was not right.
That was not what I understood by Americanism.
If I really believed Jesus when He promised,
"But seek ye first the Kingdom of God, and His righteousness;
and all these *things* shall be added unto you . . ."   *Matt.* 6:33
then I had to fulfill my part of the bargain.
And I did not believe that bribery had any place in the King-
dom or was a part of His righteousness.

So I did not take the steel construction job.
Instead I left New York City for New Jersey.
There I got a job with a gas and electric company.
We were putting down four-inch conduits across the Hudson
Tubes into Kearny and West New York.

My next job was assisting a molder in a Paterson foundry.
But during these months I was praying, asking God to show
me what He wanted me to do in this country.
I could not really believe that He had brought me from Scotland to the United States to dig my way across New Jersey
    or to fire a blast furnace.

Then came a letter from David R. Wood in Birmingham,
Alabama.
Dave had been a boyhood friend of mine in Scotland and had
emigrated the year before to the United States.
Dave wanted me to come to Birmingham.
He himself had found warm friends in the South, and he was
sure that he could get me a job on the *Birmingham News*.

One Sunday afternoon I went out on the back stoop with
Dave's letter in my hand.
It was a hot August afternoon in Elizabeth, New Jersey.
How can I ever forget?
And I prayed, I asked the Chief for directions.
        What did He want me to do?
        Was I supposed to go south?

I received the answer clearly, as clearly as my directions
had come to leave Scotland... "Yes, this is it. This is your
next step.
Go south and go immediately."

I went immediately—on a bus—with borrowed money.
And indeed that was the right step.
For, like Dave, I too found friends in the South—and a job
                    and opening doors
                    and a way to go to seminary,

a wonderful new life,
the life God had planned for me.

You cannot have experiences like that and doubt any longer
that God can move mountains—even in our day.
Maybe you do not believe that prayer changes things, but I
can assure you that I, and many others like me, know better.
Prayer changes us . . .
     and changes other people . . .
     and changes circumstances.

Too many people today have an attitude of skepticism . . .
                 or disillusionment
              or disappointment
            or frank incredulity.

The people who say "I prayed . . . and it didn't work" too often
conclude therefore that prayer is unavailing,
     or that the prayer was not heard at all . . .
     or that if He heard, God did not care.

Now there is a great mystery here, and I would not for one
moment make light of it.
There is such a thing as unanswered prayer.
The Bible tells us of some of them, and there are those among
you who have addressed sincere petitions that are as yet unanswered.

Let us face this mystery honestly.
I cannot explain it—and it would be glib and dishonest of
me to try.

I can only say that there are times when God must say "No"
to our petitions, just as fathers and mothers at times refuse the
petitions of their own children.

Let me make the point by modern analogy.

When you flick the electric-light switch in your room and the light does not come on, do you immediately conclude that it is not the nature of electricity to light up rooms?

Or that electricity plays favorites and just
does not like you enough to give you light...
therefore you will have no further use for electricity—
you are through?

No, of course not.

You know immediately that there must be some rational explanation for the failure of the light...

a faulty connection,
a broken switch,
a blown fuse,
or a burned-out bulb.

If you have prayed—and nothing happened—did you immediately conclude that prayer does not work?

Or that God does not care about you anyway?
Or that He can't be expected to know anything about
your insignificant problems and affairs?
Or bother about them if He did?

Did it ever occur to you that there might be another explanation?

Have you ever thought that maybe you had a faulty connection—were not plugged in properly to that source of divine power and love?

I can hear you say: "What do you mean by 'not plugged in properly'?

What more can one do than just pray?"

Well, think again of plugging into a socket.
You have to be sure that there is nothing wrong with the plug itself.
It could have exposed wires—it could have a short-circuit—
    and the result would be either a blown fuse . . .
        sparks and a shock . . .
or nothing at all.

We can and often do short-circuit our prayers by faults within ourselves—wrong attitudes like resentment . . .
        feelings of self-pity . . .
       envy and pride . . .
      or wrong actions.

We had better get this straight—we can't go on living a life of self-will and self-indulgence, in and out of jams, and send up a quick prayer for help and expect God to fix it all up, so that we can go on as before.

I like this definition from the Presbyterian *Shorter Catechism:*
    "Prayer is an offering up of our desires unto God, for things agreeable to His will, in the name of Christ, with confession of our sins, and thankful acknowledgement of His mercies."

Most of us have not realized that anything which will glorify God is His will.
And what Christ was telling us in the mountain-moving passage is that the circumference of things which will glorify God is wider than we think.
And mountains are of wide circumference!

Hence if moving a mountain will glorify God,

then mountain-moving is within the province of God's will.
And we can be sure that petitions concerning the physical
and spiritual health
and daily happiness
of human beings
are squarely at the center of that will.

How boldly we may pray and how absolutely certain we may
be of the glory of God is well illustrated in an event in the life
of Martin Luther.
In 1540, Luther's good friend Frederick Myconius lay dying.
Luther received a farewell letter from his friend, written with
a weak and trembling hand.

Immediately Luther sent back this reply:

"I command thee in the name of God to live, because
I still have need of thee in the work of reforming the
church . . .
The Lord will not let me hear while I live that thou art
dead, but will permit thee to survive me.
For this I am praying.
This is my will, and may my will be done, because I seek
only to glorify the name of God."

The dying man had already lost the power of speech when
this letter arrived, but within a short time he was well again.
He survived Luther by two months!

Maybe you haven't known that there is a God who is ready
and willing to do great things in you,
and through you,
and for you,
in answer to your prayers.

You will never know it until you really ask God for something
—something specific—and find out for yourself.

Is there a mountain in your life you would like removed?
Nothing is impossible with God.

> "If you, being evil know how to give good gifts unto your
> children . . .
> how much more shall your heavenly Father give the
> Holy Spirit to them that ask Him!"   *Luke* 11:13

"How much more God!"
Over and over Christ repeated these words—
"How much more God!"

"Ask, and ye shall receive, that your joy may be full."
Ask—with faith that God keeps His promises.

Ask with faith just the size of a grain of mustard seed.
     Try it out!
         Take the Lord up on His promises!

Try a little mountain-moving . . .
and you will find it the greatest adventure of your life.

·XI·

≈§ *For those who asked Peter Marshall to perform their wedding ceremony, he required—wherever possible—several conferences. As a result, there were a few occasions when he refused to marry a given couple.*

Early in his ministry, he had written his own marriage ceremony. This had been typed and pasted in on top of the printed Order for the Solemnization of Marriage in his blue leather Book of Common Worship.

This was never a routine service, quickly dispensed with. Judging by dozens of letters, many a couple regard Dr. Marshall's wedding ceremony as one of the high points of their lives.

One of these brides was the sister of an FBI agent who knew Peter well. Martha's wedding was to be a small one in the Lincoln Chapel, nothing unusual about it. Yet years later, the FBI agent—not usually given to sentimentality—was describing the scene for me:

"Dr. Marshall stood before the flower-banked altar waiting for the wedding party. It was the gladness on his face that I can never forget. There was a twinkle in his eyes, a lilt to his voice . . .

" 'Dearly beloved . . . the marriage relation when rightly understood and properly appreciated, is the most delightful, as well as the most sacred and solemn of human relations.

It is the clasping of hands, the blending of lives, and the union of hearts, that two may walk together up the hill of life to meet the dawn—together bearing life's burdens . . . discharging its duties . . . sharing its joys and sorrows.'

"Some of the service he must have written just for Martha and Dick. I was so fascinated by the vibrancy of his voice, the buoyant joy that lifted every sentence to give it a memorable quality I had never before heard in a wedding ceremony.

" 'Marriage is much more than moonlight and roses, much more than the singing of love songs and the whispering of vows of undying affection. In our day, it is by many lightly regarded, and by many as lightly discarded. But marriage will ever remain, in the sight of God an eternal union, made possible only by the gift of love which God alone can bestow.

" 'Therefore we are still entitled to say that true marriages are made in Heaven, because that which, above *all* things, makes a marriage true and happy comes only from God. . . .'

"I hold dear to my heart the things Dr. Marshall told my sister and my brother-in-law:

" 'Remember Martha, that it was Love that gave you this man—and you, Dick, this woman—not this ceremony. . . Your marriage must stand and endure, not by the authority of the marriage license, nor by the strength of the wedding certificate—for these are only pieces of paper —but by the strength of your love and the endurance of your faith in each other and in Jesus Christ, without which no marriage can be truly happy. . . .'

"Then Dr. Marshall asked that Martha and Dick look at each other, rather than at him, as they spoke their vows. And as I stood there hearing those ancient, lovely words, In plenty and in want, in joy and in sorrow, as long as we both shall live, I knew why that moment would be unforgettable —not because of any particular words that Dr. Marshall had strung together, however fine—but because he had brought with him into the chapel the joyful presence of Him who attended the wedding feast and who blesses all true romance."

THE ELECT LADY

D O you believe that true marriages are still made in heaven? That God cares about whom you marry? ...

That somewhere there is a particular person meant for you? Or do you think that such idealism is pious nonsense?

These are pertinent questions.
For you cannot believe in God the Father as Jesus revealed Him, and not believe that He cares about you as an individual. And if God is interested in you and in what you do, then would He not be interested in whom you marry?

Perhaps you think that falling in love is enough.
But we are so often wrong about love ...

Many of us do not recognize it when it comes.

Many of us mistake sexual attraction alone for love. Surely here—with regard to marriage—we need God's help more than in anything else.

Is not the proof of that the dark shadow of divorce that lies across every hearthstone?
One marriage in every four now ends in divorce.
There is evidence that soon it will be one marriage in every three.

You need God's help in the realm of courtship and marriage because you are disillusioned and lost without Him.
Many already have tasted of a society which is debauched.
You see divorce organized as big business.
> You see society's daughters and sons taught to drink at an earlier and earlier age.
> You see mothers who covet popularity for their daughters at whatever price, push them out into society like tempting bargains placed in a store window.

Some of you have tasted of the fleshpots.
You are prematurely old,
> not so much in experience
> as in disappointment.
Already you have haunted hearts.

Your defense against these wrongs is often an assumption of indifference.
You cultivate a veneer of apathy and nonchalance as a shield against being hurt.

But underneath the veneer there lurks a wistful, poignant quest for some kind of enduring values, an idealism tested by experience.
You must have solid ground beneath you, and this is precisely what Jesus Christ offers.

When you refuse to let Him direct your dating,

your courtship,
your marriage;
you are cheating yourself of one of the greatest gifts of all.
How can I dramatize for you what you are missing?

The world loves romance and seeks it everywhere.
Nine out of every ten songs are about love.
Sex is exploited to sell everything from spark plugs to hair
tonic.
Hollywood has worn the subject thin . . .
and thinner . . .
until there is no substance left, only tawdriness.

The romance offered by the world is as a ring set with dime-
store glass.
The romance God offers you is a pure and flashing diamond.
Synthetic . . . The real thing.
Ephemeral . . . Eternal.
Mockery . . . Fulfillment.
That is the difference; think well before you choose.

But understand that you may have God's help with your
romance only on His terms.
First of all, He insists that His children dream big.
Because He wants our happiness, He will settle for no cheap
compromises,
no tawdry substitutes,
only the best for any of His.

God demands idealism with regard to sex.
Let us frankly face the fact that the keenest of all problems,
the sharpest of all temptations
is to compromise personal purity and chastity.

That is where the battleground is.
And so—with no apologies and no equivocation—I challenge
you to Christ's ideal for sex.

Dr. Harry Emerson Fosdick once confided in a sermon to his
congregation at the Riverside Church, New York, how he
battled this as a young man.
He decided to force himself to face the question of what use
he wanted to make of sex in his life . . .
Did he want a Christian home with its deep fidelities and
satisfactions,
      or a loose life of sensuality?
He was reasonably sure that he could not have both.

He chose!
In order to make that choice clear-cut and definite, he sat
down and wrote a letter to the girl he was going to marry—
      even though he had never met her.
The letter expressed his confidence that his wife-to-be was
waiting for him somewhere,
      that at the right moment they would meet,
         that in the meantime, he was going to keep his fidelity
      to her as true as if she were already his bride.

At the time Dr. Fosdick spoke about this to his congregation,
his wedding day was some forty years in the past.
In retrospect, looking back over long years, he could say,
               "That decision cost . . ."
          Of course it cost!
"But how grateful I am for it, that I did not make the other
choice and surrender all the deep and sacred satisfaction of
these lovely years for a mess of pottage." [7]

Of course, those "lovely years" . . .
    "the deep and sacred satisfaction" . . .
would not have been possible had not the girl waiting for
Harry Emerson Fosdick shared his idealism.

Perhaps we need to look again at what Christ's concept of
womanhood is.
The emancipation of women did not begin in the twentieth
century.
It began with Christianity, for Jesus Christ was the first to
usher women into a new place in human relations.
Jesus accorded woman a dignity she had never known before
and crowned her with a glory, so that she might be revered,
protected, and loved.

The symbol of purity and chastity has traditionally been a
white rose.
I wonder if it would not be more accurate to choose a gardenia
. . . because the gardenia with its fragrance and the velvet of its
petals cannot endure to be handled . . .
                treated roughly
              or bruised at all,
for its pure white petals will reveal every telltale mark of
handling.

Jesus Christ both challenges you and promises to help you,
so that when you stand before the altar to whisper your
wedding vows—both you and your bridegroom will be able to
lay upon that alter a gardenia without spot or blemish, for
what is desirable in a bride is just as desirable in a bridegroom.

Any temporary sacrifice or renunciation is a small price to pay
for the achievement of ideals which will yield later in your
marriage, dividends of peace, of joy, and of happiness.

There was a time when many a bride brought her white offering to the altar but knew that it lay there alone.
For there prevailed the iniquitous "double standard."
This was the philosophy that permitted,
               even encouraged
a young man to sow his wild oats . . .
with the excuse that he was only young once.

So he might step over moral bounds in sexual adventures, but
when he settled down, he had a right to choose for a wife a
girl who was sweet, pure and chaste.

You can be sure that Christ's standard is no double standard.
Today's girls are quite right to reject it.
But the standards which many of you have substituted are not
Christ's either.

Today's women have interpreted emancipation as the freedom
to smoke like a man,
     to drink like a man,
          to use rough language, to swear,
               to work like a man,
                    to treat sex as loosely as a man.

Women have copied the vices of men—in the name of
progress!
But it is never progress to go in a downward direction.
It is not progress to lose ideals, to lower morality.
No girl ever became more desirable by losing her femininity,
                                        or her innocence.

I have never heard a man say that a girl's mouth was prettier
with a cigarette hanging out of it,

or that her hair smelled divinely of tobacco smoke.
I have read no poetry rhapsodizing over a girl's smutty joke.

Will a modern child—grown-up—remember some faint unforgettable fragrance which always seemed to be in his
mother's hair?
Or will he remember instead the odor of scotch on her breath?

Will he tenderly recall that day he rushed unbidden into her
bedroom to find her on her knees beside her favorite chair?
Or will he remember her, dressed in slacks, putting off his
eager questions while she poured cocktails for her noisy guests?

Perhaps today's women will not feel so triumphant about their
"emancipation" when they realize that men no longer feel as
romantic about girls as did their grandfathers.
If something sweet and mysterious has been lost, this so-called
equality is a poor exchange for the privilege of being different,
of being a woman.

Is it too late?
What of those who have already tasted of this debauched
society?
Is it too late for Christ's idealism?

No, it is not.
Christ gave us a deeper concept of purity than anyone else
has ever conceived.
He added a new dimension to it.

He taught us that purity is not just for the untouched,
the untried
the untempted.

The knight who rides past with shield bright and armor un-

stained and unspotted may never have been in the fight.
The clean shield proves nothing.

That person who has never felt the temptation to do
anything ignoble,
to lower his ideals,
to listen to the honeyed whispers of sensuality . . .
that person whose life has been so sheltered that he has never
felt blowing on his cheeks the scorching blasts of passion is as
a ship that has never been launched.

That ship may be seaworthy—or it may not.
The sheltered person may have strength—or he may not.

Jesus Christ was too realistic . . .
knew human nature too well,
not to realize that each of us is tempted.
Not one of us remains untainted by impurity of deed or
thought.

And so in God's eyes the pure vessel is not only that which
remains untouched.
Pure is the vessel also which the Master has cleansed . . .
in whom His spirit abides to keep us cleansed.
Else He could never have forgiven and accepted
Mary of Magdala . . .
Zaccheus . . .
the woman taken in adultery . . .
the Gadarene demoniac . . .
Joanna, the wife of Herod's steward, Chuza,
the woman with the alabaster box of ointment . . .

He is the only One who claims to be able to forgive and to
cleanse.

Over and over, He provides that glorious new beginning for haunted hearts.
Always His word is what it was to that nameless woman long ago:
"Go and sin no more.
Make a clean break with whatever it is that has dragged you down."

In order to get God's help with your dreams of romance, you will have to live out your faith that He is able to guide you,
live it out day by day,
episode by episode.
It has to be a practical faith.

You should talk over with Christ the questions that trouble you—the perplexities of dating,
the constant head-on collision between your ideals and your wish to be popular and accepted.

These matters you discuss constantly with your friends, do you not?
Then why not with Christ?
He has more wisdom to give you about dating than any of your friends could ever have.

Is it possible that society is on the wrong track today with regard to courtship and marriage?
Many sociologists, psychologists, and marriage counselors are rapidly coming to that conclusion.

They point out that our western dating patterns go back no farther than World War I...
that we romanticists, who scorn the "arranged" Oriental or European marriage, need to take a new, hard look at the

tragedies and heartaches which our hit-and-miss courtship, our customs are bringing.

We see society's sons and daughters pairing off at an earlier and earlier age . . .
We watch a shocking kind of mutal exploitation:
> The boy trying to exploit the girl sexually . . .
> the girl exploiting the boy financially . . .
>> *exploiting* being simply another word for selfishness.

And so the sociologists are convinced that we need a profound and creative revolution, if we are to save the home as an institution.
What they have not led us on to see is that the revolution must be in our hearts:
> no longer what can I *get* from the marriage I seek,
> but rather what can I *give?*

For you girls this may come down to some difficult questions. For example, many girls today are unwilling to make of their marriage a full-time job.

There is a conflict between hard economic facts and the dreams of a home in the hearts of many young women.
But when a girl is unwilling to give up her name,
her career,
> her own selfish ambitions for her husband's sake,
> she had better stay out of marriage.

Beginning with what is often simply greed for a larger income, greed for *things*, material possessions, household gadgets, for many young women the accepted practice of working after marriage has distorted their concept of what marriage really is. In Christ's eyes, true love must be ever a giving of oneself.

In the case of a wife, bearing her husband's name,
    seeking to please him,
        creating with her hands a home for him,
           bearing his children.

The creation of a home where memories abide does not depend on possessions.
Gracious living is created by loving hands,
                by a tranquil mind,
                    a heart in which God dwells,
                    a soul which knows beauty.
Calmness,
    serenity
      faith
        contentment
        tenderness,
manifesting themselves in the way a woman goes quietly about her household tasks.

Such qualities are not furthered by hard, competitive days in the office . . .
by the hurried preparation of meals after working hours with no time left for the children.

The women I know who are the happiest, whose homes are a joy to enter, are the ones who have made a clear-cut decision. Often at economic sacrifice, they have decided that they cannot create a real home on less than full time.

But this kind of giving is possible only if there is a reciprocal giving on the part of the husband—"Husbands, love your wives"—not in terms of a popular song moaned into a microphone,
    not with a box of candy,

or a corsage twice a year,
not with any of the sentimental slush that is so often a counter-
feit for love.

But "love your wives even as Christ also loved the church, and
gave himself for it..."   *Ephesians* 6:25
There is a concept of a husband's love!
That means something.

Look at Christ on the cross—there for us husbands is the
ideal...
There is Love giving Himself for His bride...
     self-sacrificing love—knowing no bounds,
   having no restraint,
  love even unto death.
Such a love can come only from God.

I have found that no marriage ceremony, however beautiful
and meaningful, will make two selfish people, governed by
self-will, into an unselfish couple.
There is nothing magical about the marriage ceremony.

No problem which any married couple can have is beyond
solution if they are willing to get down on their knees together
and ask God what to do about it.
It is not a question of what the husband wants—or what the
wife wants—but always, what does God want?

So many children have an imaginary character with whom they
live and gravely discuss everything.
A certain mother heard her five-year-old son carrying on a
conversation under the kitchen table with his imaginary play-
mate:
    "Who's the boss in your home, Johnny?" asked the un-
    seen guest. "Your father or your mother?"

"Neither," said Johnny. "God's boss in our home."
Here was a fortunate little boy who had seen his parents reach
out in the most practical way beyond self-will to find God's
will.

And that must be the pattern from the beginning of your dating right on into the home you will create, if you are to find the
romance that God has planned for you.
For human beings vary little from century to century.
The manifestations of self-will change, but not the selfishness.
Dreams linger in every heart—along with the temptations to
compromise those dreams.

But God can change our self-will, so that we can find the love
He has planned for us.
That is what happened to a woman I shall call Mary.

Her home is in a Southern city.
I know it well, for I have been entertained there often.
She is a woman of some means—her heart and her home
always open—with a hospitality that ministers both to the
tired body and the discouraged soul of many a guest.

I always think of her as the modern counterpart of the "elect
lady" of Ephesus to whom John wrote his Second Epistle.
"Elect lady . . ." What a charming way to speak of a mother
for whom the years have woven the brocade of gentleness she
now wears, always with her slow smile of understanding love!

Yet in the modern elect lady's past lay a surprising story.
I heard it from her own lips . . .
Years before, when she was a young mother, a three-year-old
son had been drowned.

Her grief was compounded by bitterness toward her husband
because the boy had been in his care for the day.

With the bitterness, a process of disintegration set in.
Mary had been a meticulous housekeeper and a fine cook;
                              now she no longer cared.
Dust and disarray took over her home . . .
              In the garden were weeds and rank growth, like the
              debris piling up and up in her heart . . .

Nor did she care any longer about how she looked until—
until one morning a woman whom she had never seen before
knocked on her front door,
        marched into the living room,
              announced that she was in love with Mary's husband,
              John.

"Somehow I got through that dreadful scene," Mary told me,
"and got the woman out of the house.
Then I went to the kitchen, poured a cup of strong coffee,
                    sat down for a good cry
                    and a long hard look at myself.

"Suddenly a bit of Scripture came out of dim recesses of
memory:
        'See to it that no root of bitterness spring up and cause
        trouble, and by it the many become defiled—'
"I saw it all then . . .
I had let the roots of bitterness about Johnny's death grow up
and fill my heart until there was no room left for love.
My bitterness had defiled our marriage and our home.

"Then I thought of the other woman, and I got mad.
How could I forgive that?

I cried some more ... threw a cup across the kitchen where it
went crashing against the wall ...
     beat my fists on the table ... screamed, 'I won't ... I
won't.'

"But all the time a quiet voice inside me was saying, 'You
must. You must forgive.
     There is no other way.'

"Then I walked over to that large mirror there in the dining
room to take a good look at myself.
I was horrified at what I saw ...
Once I had been considered the belle of our town.
And now—here was a woman with disillusioned eyes ...
               hard lines around her mouth ...
                 hair stringy and unkempt ...
No wonder my husband had been attracted to another
woman."

My hostess sighed ... and smiled her slow smile, remembering.
"Everything came out all right.
Christ came again into our home.
John and I had twelve years together before he died—
             near-perfect years, the happiest of all.
I had a second baby boy—always a joy to us.
He is now a physician in Kansas City."

I looked about me at the shining mahogany,
     the freshly starched curtains fluttering in the night breeze,
        the roses in the silver vase, grown in the garden outside,
          the portrait of John ...
The artist had captured on canvas the face of a happy husband.

And in imagination I saw behind Mary's shoulder so many

elect ladies who are called by God to create homes in which
love dwells . . .
A cottage in Georgia with wisteria trailing over the porch . . .
    a trailer home with a very young mother . . .
        a tiny apartment . . .
           a split-level in suburbia . . .
               a square white house under an arch of elms in a
               New England village . . .
                   a ranch house overlooking the ocean on the
                   Monterey Peninsula.

I thought of the mothers who preside over these homes,
               modern women, not at all like Whistler's mother.
They know all about germs and sanitation,
          vitamins and food values,
          formulas and schedules.

They are tireless in providing for the physical needs of their
children—these modern mothers—
        ambitious for their future intellectual life—
        eager for their proper social development.
They will chauffeur their children anywhere, to dancing classes
. . . Scout meetings . . . the dentist . . . the movies.
They will attend PTA meetings and forums endlessly.
But as for spiritual nourishment for their children, many of
them have never given it a thought.

How could they—when they themselves do not know God in
a real and personal way?
They read the best-sellers, child psychology books—but the
Bible scarcely ever.
Perhaps it never occurs to them that God has wisdom and
guidance to give them about their marriage and their children.
Yet how our tired old world needs parents who are willing to

add to their knowledge of economics and sociology and psychology a knowledge of God.

We need young women who would rather be called "elect ladies" than "the smartest young matron in town."
The nation cries out for couples who will build true homes—
whether they live in two rooms or ten ...
whether starched white organdy curtains
or silk damask draperies hang at the windows.
You can have a home like that, if you will recognize that God is the greatest asset to romance there is.
He thought it up in the first place!
Reach for His idealism, so that your home may be built on spiritual foundations,
with your family life oiled by the grace of God.

"Where there is faith, there is peace;
Where there is peace, there is love;
Where there is love, there is God,
Where there is God, there is no need."

Only in such homes can we build the better world of which we dream.

·XII·

❧ *The two girls found seats near the front of the church. After the last rich notes of Bach's "Here Yet Awhile" from the Saint Matthew Passion died away, Dr. Marshall arose slowly, looked up at the choir for a moment, as if smiling his gratitude for the sixty-eight loyal young voices.*

Betty was thinking how much she liked the way he conducted a service. He never rushed from one part to another, but often sat in his high-backed chair for a leisurely moment, thoroughly relaxed, as if he too were worshiping—drinking in the refreshing quietness. Under the spell of such periods of silence, Betty could feel the brood of ills of the week past—all the noise and confusion of her government office—slipping away. Peace would come stealing into her heart. She had come to look forward to these services.

But now the musical voice from the pulpit was beginning. With a sigh of contentment she settled back in the pew. The sermon was about death—and immortality.

After the service on the way back to their 16th Street apartment, Marion said suddenly, "You know, Dr. Marshall's sermon today did something for me. I've been afraid of death all my life, ever since my collie Mac died when I was six. You've heard me talk about old Mac. Well, after hearing that sermon, I know I'll never be afraid of death again. It's great to be free of that fear."

Betty smiled at her friend. "I know. Dr. Marshall's con-

fidence is catching. He makes death sound like an exciting adventure, like going to a glad reunion."

On Friday of that week, Dr. Marshall received a letter which read:

Dear Dr. Marshall,

Last Sunday a friend and I heard you preach on death! Afterwards she told me and my roommates that you had made death such a beautiful natural experience that for the first time in her life, she was no longer afraid to die.

She—Marion—was killed Wednesday in an automobile trip to Florida. It happened on the highway between Macon and Dalton, Georgia. She died instantly. Because she was so young (twenty-four), so full of life, so happy, it has been a deep shock to all of us who knew her. One of our greatest comforts has been to recall her comments on "Rendezvous in Samarra" which released her from the fear of death.

May God keep you as His comforter to us, who need Him so much.

Sincerely,
Elizabeth Durand

One Sunday a few months later—December 7, 1941— Peter Marshall and I drove to Annapolis where Peter was to speak at the Naval Academy. At the last moment he had an overwhelming feeling that he should change his announced topic and instead preach the sermon on death and immortality:

For what is your life? It is even a vapor that appeareth for a little while and then vanisheth away.

On the way back to Washington that afternoon came the stunning announcement of the Japanese attack on Pearl Harbor. The nation was at war. Within a matter of days many of the young men to whom Dr. Marshall had just proclaimed his ringing assurance of life after death, would be on the high seas. Some would not return. "Rendezvous in Samarra" provided prophetic strengthening for some of the midshipmen in their time of need. I know this because Peter received several letters from distant places thanking him for his message that fateful Sunday morning.

RENDEZVOUS IN SAMARRA

"For what is your life? It is even a vapor, that appeareth for a little time, and then vanisheth away." *James* 4:14

Whenever my mother spoke of plans for the future, she always added—even in her letters—the phrase "God willing."
This is not just a pious cliché.
It is the clear recognition that her future was in God's hands.

The apostle James would approve this viewpoint.
For in speaking of human life as being a vapor, James was warning those who make great assumptions for the future with never a thought of God . . .
"I shall go to such and such a city . . ."
"I shall be there for a year . . ."
"These are our business plans."

Such as these do not recognize that the issue of life and death is in the hands of God.

Indeed, for every one of us, life is a fragile thing.

The messenger that summons us into the larger room may be
visible or invisible . . .
expected or unexpected . . .

The summons is just as imperative!

A matter of seconds and yards, that is all that was between you and a crash on the highway the other day.

A tiny microbe—so small that your naked eye could not see it —has called many a man away from the broken toys of this life.

History is filled with dramatic illustrations of the fragility of life and the unexpectedness with which the summons may come.

Perhaps no illustration is more vivid than the *Hindenburg* disaster in 1937 as it was described by Dale Harrison of the Associated Press.

It was the afternoon of May the sixth.
    Lightning flashed the sullen clouds.
        Thunder rolled up and down the skies.
        Rain fell . . .
        It was a dismal evening.

Out of the east floated the silver *Hindenburg* . . .
        like a graceful cigar . . .
        Germany's pride—a haughty triumph over nature.

For though the thunder clapped and the lightning flashed viciously, the silver thing rode softly on . . .
    unperturbed and unharmed.

She was late . . . many hours late, for the weather was bad and she was cautious.

Better late than never!
Men and women waited at Lakehurst—impatient.
They were anxious for the *Hindenburg* to come down, for they
were going to London for the coronation.

The *Hindenburg* lazed along . . . Let the storm diminish.
Let the wind die . . . then she would come down.
No need to hurry.
There were ninety-nine human beings aboard.
The lightning grew weary of its futile strikes
at the silver monster.
    The thunder crawled off . . . grumbling.
      The rain became desultory . . .
      The clouds broke ranks.

The *Hindenburg* began talking: "All is well," she said over her
radio, "I am coming down."
She was mistress of the sky.
On the ground newsmen and photographers loitered with
movie-camera men and field officials.

Covering a *Hindenburg* arrival had become a dull assignment.
Nothing ever happened.

The *Hindenburg* pointed her nose to the ground.
From her sleek sides threads of rope dangled, reaching for the
handclasp of the ground crew.
Rain still fell, but softly now.
Passengers poked laughing faces from cabin windows.
      Some waved handkerchiefs.
        There were children at those windows too.

She dipped majestically—the haughty airship of silk
                    and steel
                    and dangerous gas.

It was six twenty-three.
From somewhere jumped a spark—a spark so small you could
hardly see it.
And in less time than it takes to tell, the *Hindenburg* exploded.

Flames leaped from her middle—flames of red and yellow
                    wrapped in black and purple smoke.
She hung there for an instant—as though reluctant to die.

From the flaming ship bodies dropped.
It was forty, fifty,
        or one hundred feet to the ground.
No one knew exactly how far it was.
It is difficult to be mathematical when men and women are
falling screaming to their deaths.
On the ground there were shouts to the ground crew:
                        "Run for your lives."

Men and women dropped like flaming torches
                or like sparks in the indifferent rain.
Some lay where they fell, forever still.
Others, incredibly, rose up and staggered away.

Many came through it safely . . . sixty-three escaped . . .
                        however incredible it seems.
Sixty-three emerged alive—scorched
                burned
                shocked
                speechless
            horrified . . . but alive.
A fool would call it "luck."

What shall we call it?
Thirty-six people died—in an instant.

At the last there was a feeble flame.
It crawled skyward and lost itself in the blackness of the night.[8]

Yes, James, life is a vapor which disappears
                    slips from our grasp
             all in an instant.

But most of us never think of death or dying.
    We act as though we had a long lease on life ...
      As though we had immunity somehow ...
        As though that cold and clammy hand would never
        be laid on our hearts
or the shrouds of that dread messenger never brush against us.
It is a foolish attitude to take about an inevitability.
For death is life's greatest, perhaps its only, certainty.

They betray not only their fear but also their ignorance who
say, "Let's not talk about death or dying.
    Let's talk of something more pleasant."

Of course, that is true to our modern pattern.
We are not willing to face unpleasantness, and when we are
presented with facts we do not like to hear, we call them
"propaganda" and dismiss them.

But what is there to fear?
What contemplation could be more pleasant than what awaits
us after death?
Here we have pain—and partings
                  tears and tragedies
                work and weariness
                    heartaches—disillusionments.
We grow old ... our eyes dimming ... hair graying ...
Desperately we try to camouflage the betraying years.

I assure you that the life to come is infinitely more pleasant to contemplate than any of that.
It is more pleasant than reading our daily papers with their stories of crime and human wickedness
cruelty and violence
sordid tales of passion and greed.
It is more pleasant than the thought of atomic warfare.

For if the Bible is true and Christ has not deceived us, there awaits just behind the curtain a life that will never end
a life of beauty and peace and love
a life of reunion with loved ones
a life to be lived in the very Presence of God.

There will be no more pain,
no more sorrow, nor tears,
nor crying,
nor parting,
nor death after death.
Age shall not weary them, nor the years erode.
We shall enter into that for which we were created.
It shall be the journey's end for the heart and all its hopes.

And yet there are those among us whose actions—let us eat, drink, and be merry, for tomorrow we die—suggest that they believe in no better hereafter.

There never was a time when the conviction of immortality was more needed than in this day when materialism has so exalted present life as to make it all-important.

People whose vision of death is earthbound remind me of the

caterpillar crawling along the warm earth, imagining that heaven for him will be an endless row of cabbages.

Then one day a second caterpillar with a more philosophical turn of mind would say to his friend: "You know, I believe that some day you and I will no longer have to crawl along the ground, but might even fly over that fence. What is more, we will not be puncturing cabbage leaves with our neat little holes and stuffing ourselves full of green stuff, but we might be sipping dew and living on honey."

His friend, fastening on him incredulous beady eyes, might reply: "I knew this night life would get you."
Or, solicitously he might say: "Poor old chap, you have been working too hard lately. You've cracked under the strain."

And when the time comes for him to "die," his caterpillar friends gather round—and extol his virtues.

"He was a connoisseur of cabbage. He was a good old caterpillar—now this is the end."
And so he is buried in a shroud—a chrysalis shroud that spins upon the twig, a shriveled, dry grave.

And yet, by and by, on a summer morning
the grave bursts open,
        the chrysalis breaks, and out of it emerges a moist,
            trembling, lovely thing that hoists into the fragrant air
delicate sails of beauty.

As they dry and gather strength, the butterfly becomes aware of a new world.
And when the gossamer wings are dry and their colors are fast,
        the butterfly takes off and, fluttering, sails over the fence
        to sip the dew and taste the succulent honey.

In our superior wisdom, we know which caterpillar is right. We know that he goes to sleep a caterpillar and wakes up a butterfly.

But do we know as much about our own beautiful destinies after the long sleep?

There are none on whom the Reaper will not call.
Death does come to the archbishop,
>> to the king in his palace,
>> >> the beggar by the roadside,
>> >> and the rat in his hole.

But persons are not blown out like candles in the wind.
Infinity surrounds us.
> Is it dead?
>> Is it empty?
>>> Is it a shivering void where nothing lives?
Is it a cold space into which we are launched to evaporate and disappear?

So we ask our questions and receive our answers.
Do we think our transformation will be any less beautiful and startling than caterpillar into butterfly?
We have the witness of Personality—the sense of Identity greater than the universe.
We are aware of a star;
we cannot conceive of a star being aware of us.

We know that we are here for a reason, otherwise earth would become a mere picture house, and life the stupid walking to and fro of shadows on a screen . . .
Religion would then be a silly symphony of jazz played beside deathbeds to keep idiots quiet, to dull their jangled nerves as they are about to plunge off into nothingness.

You can stand before a glass case in the anthropology wing of
any good museum and see laid out in a row of saucers the con-
stituent elements of the human body.

There is so much phosphorus
                    so much silicon
              iron
            carbon
          lime
        water, and so forth ...
Enough iron, I believe, to make a half-dozen tenpenny nails ...
Enough lime to whitewash an ordinary chicken coop ...
Enough phosphorus to tip the heads of a thousand matches.

There, they will tell you, is the human body—
What? There you are?
There I am? ... No!
That may be my body—it is not I.
That may be the house in which I lived, but it is not the
tenant.

Moreover, the physicists and anatomists tell us that the cell
tissue and structure of the body changes every seven or eight
years—is completely rebuilt, re-created.

So "you" are not your body—for you are the same individual
who has seen several such cycles—yet you remain the same
person conscious of continuous existence.

Nor are "you" your brain.
Your brain cells change in every cycle of reconstruction.
Then how does it happen that I remember what I thought and
did and said with the old vanished brain of twenty years ago?

My memory tells me that I am the same "I" in spite of all those changes in my brain.

Parts of the body—a finger, an arm, a leg—may be amputated.
Yet the person, the "I," is still there.
The violin will be laid down some day . . .
The old refrains that skillful hands have plucked from its heart will be heard no more—but the musician will still be alive.

No half-mad humorist tossed the world aloft and left its destiny to chance . . .
No infinite juggler threw into space the ball of his creation and walked away heedless of where it fell.
No blind groper in the mists of creation let a handful of dust trickle through his fingers to fall in a shower of sparks and turn into stars.

"The meek shall inherit the earth," Christ said, but He did not mean six feet of it, not a hole in the ground.
The grave is not their final heritage.
There are a thousand insane things easier to believe than this.

Human personality will survive, else God would be the capricious universal joker who created toys in His own image so that He might break them . . .
        laugh at their disfigurements . . .
and sweep them into the garbage cans of His own caprice.

To believe this makes life a jumbled mystery,
                        aimless and futile
                    human effort a farce
                    human hope a mockery
human sorrow the cue for the crackling laughter of insane gods.

Yet where can we find the reassurance the heart seeks?

Let us honestly face the fact that all the
    arguments—philosophical and otherwise,
        analogies—however close and persuasive,
            testimony—all of it that psychic research can so far produce, are still not conclusive evidence for immortality.
They leave us in the twilight of an excruciating uncertainty.

The only proof—the final convincing proof—is to be found in Jesus Christ.
In Him is all the authority needed to garrison your heart when the waters threaten to engulf and the darkness closes in.

How? Because He has proved, and stands ready to prove, that what we can experience with our five senses is not the only reality,
    indeed, is far less real than the actualities in the realm of the Spirit.

It was through His resurrection that Christ demonstrated this to His first disciples.
These men and women had not expected Christ to rise from the dead.
When His battered body was taken down from the Cross, their hopes and their dreams had already died with Him.
For He had said that He was God incarnate in human flesh.
Surely God cannot die . . . and the fact was that He was *dead*.

Therefore when the news came thirty-six hours later that His body was gone,
    that He had been seen alive,
they were shocked, bewildered.
At first, they flatly refused to credit such an idle tale.

But then, as one by one and finally in groups they saw and
experienced His presence for themselves, they were forced to
believe that Christ was indeed alive.
It was unaccountable, but stupendous!
What else in life mattered beside news like that!

So they shouted it across continents,
        blazoned it over land and sea,
                cried it, sang it, preached it, exulted in it.
Read the flaming words of those first preachers in the Acts
of the Apostles and you will see that the "good news" of
apostolic preaching was not Jesus' life—but His death;
                        not His ethic—but His resurrection.

These first disciples knew that human personality would survive . . . because One who went into the grave and beyond, had
come back to say:

    "Because I live, ye shall live also.
        Whosoever believeth in Me shall not perish but have
        eternal life . . .
        Whosoever liveth and believeth in Me shall never die."

But then, when we go beyond Christ's ringing assurances, we
are somewhat startled to find that He does not give us more
details of what we can expect behind the curtain.
I am convinced that His reticence is based not on either lack
of knowledge or on His disinclination to tell us
but on our lack of capacity to receive it.
How would you describe to a deaf mute the Fifth Symphony . . .
                or the sound of rain pattering down . . .
            or a birdsong?
Have you ever tried describing a sunset to someone born blind?
How would you begin?

Then how could Jesus have conveyed to us the reality that lies ahead of us when there is no analogy within the range of our knowledge?

He invited us rather to a different sort of proof, to the extraordinary adventure of entering into immortality for ourselves here and now, by experiencing—
even as did those first disciples—
the fact of His aliveness.
For don't you see that no fishermen and tax-collectors and housewives—no matter how persuasive—could ever have won converts to Christianity merely on their say-so?
What happened was that an increasing number of men and women themselves met Jesus Christ.

Yes, this can happen today too.
Yes, it has happened to me—and to many another.
And this—only this—is the final proof of immortality.

An old legend tells of a merchant in Bagdad who one day sent his servant to the market.
Before very long the servant came back, white and trembling, and in great agitation said to his master:
"Down in the market place I was jostled by a woman in the crowd, and when I turned around I saw it was Death that jostled me.
She looked at me and made a threatening gesture.
Master, please lend me your horse, for I must hasten away to avoid her.
I will ride to Samarra and there I will hide, and Death will not find me."

The merchant lent him his horse and the servant galloped away in great haste.

Later the merchant went down to the market place and saw
Death standing in the crowd.
He went over to her and asked,
> "Why did you frighten my servant this morning?
> Why did you make a threatening gesture?"

"That was not a threatening gesture," Death said.
"It was only a start of surprise.
I was astonished to see him in Bagdad, for I have an appointment with him tonight in Samarra."

Each of us has an appointment in Samarra.
But that is cause for rejoicing—not for fear,
provided we have put our trust in Him who alone holds
> the keys of life and death.

For at last, each of us comes back to the strongest argument of all—the Love that in earth's greatest mystery clothed itself in clay like our own,
> and, dying, left the low door of the grave unlatched,
> > so that God could come into our sorrows . . .
> > so that a loving Father could speak
> > to the earth's dumb anguish
of the Glorious Day beyond our dying sun.

NOTES

Dr. Marshall always went into the pulpit with a complete sermon manuscript. These were typed in the unusual format he had devised, the blank verse, stair-step style now familiar to the many readers of *Mr. Jones, Meet the Master* and *The First Easter*. Sometime during his Washington ministry, he destroyed many earlier sermons. Nevertheless at the time of his death, about six hundred sermon manuscripts were left.

Since these were prepared for oral delivery only, considerable editing has been necessary. In some instances, where there were several sermons written during the years on the same topic, I have used material from two, sometimes three messages, in every instance being guided by what I felt Peter would have done himself had he published the sermons during his lifetime.

Biblical quotations are confined to the King James (which remained Dr. Marshall's favorite) and a few from Moffatt's translation, which he sometimes used. And, as in earlier books, the reader will find instances where he paraphrased and elaborated on Scripture—one of his oft-used devices for interpreting favorite passages to his listeners. All scriptural references are given in the text except where the quotation is a phrase or brief sentence.

For me the sermons presented here bring back many memories—of the man and of the occasions on which the sermons were delivered. I have included a few of these memories in the brief introduction to each sermon.

[1] Jean's mother thought I would like to see the theme, and sent it to me shortly after Dr. Marshall's death. She was right—I treasure it.

[2] Paraphrased from Montague, C. E., *Rough Justice*, Doubleday & Company, Inc., New York, 1926. Used with permission.

[3] This reminiscence was part of a memorable letter which I received late in July 1953 from the Reverend David Simpson, then pastor of the Second Presbyterian Church of Fort Smith, Arkansas. David had just finished reading *A Man Called Peter*. The book had sparked "a reliving of Peter's and my seminary days."

[4] Paraphrased from Remarque, Erich Maria, *All Quiet on the Western Front*, Little, Brown & Company, Boston, 1929. Used with permission.

[5] The poem "High Flight," by Pilot-Officer John Gillespie Magee, Jr., R.C.A.F., is reprinted with the permission of his mother, Mrs. John Gillespie Magee.

[6] Lewis, C. S., *The Case for Christianity*, The Macmillan Company, New York, 1943, p. 40; and Geoffrey Bles, Ltd., London. Used with permission.

[7] Fosdick, Harry Emerson, *On Being Fit to Live With*, Harper & Row, New York, 1947, pp. 54–55. Used with permission.

[8] The Dale Harrison Story of *Hindenburg* disaster is used by permission of the Associated Press.